The Edupreneur

Your Blueprint To Jumpstart And Scale Your Education Business

Dr. Will Deyamport, III

ISBN: 978-1-959347-42-2

Contents

Acknowledgments

All praise is due to Allah (SWT) for the blessing of life and for this opportunity. None of this is possible without His (SWT) Will.

I also want to thank my wife for her 20 years of support and for being a champion of my work.

Lastly, I want to thank Dr. Sarah Thomas for believing in my pivot and rocking with me when others jumped when I shifted to entrepreneurial thinking and financial literacy education.

Foreword

It is all about our connections. We start by reaching out to one person and then continue to build a support system, a network, from that initial contact. We learn from one another. Perhaps we share our ideas or dream big. At times, we ask for help or confide in others about our desire to make a change. That change might involve shifting from the classroom, from our roles as educators, and transitioning into something else within education. Or, perhaps even undertaking something completely different.

But why? We wish to make an impact and push ourselves to do more. Not merely for our personal growth, but because we believe, deep down, that we have something more to offer that can help others. Something that can also help us.

We might aspire to do more with what we have. Perhaps it is our ideas, the advice we provide, our ability to listen, or specialized knowledge that we possess. Each of us has something. We might not realize it. Within our passion to do more, we also have doubts. Can I make a difference? Do I have what it takes? What am I doing that is so unique, or needed, or sustainable? Where do I begin? And what if I fail? Is it worth it?

These are questions we all ask ourselves.

We are all unique and talented, with our own methods of performing the work that we do. Each of us has a niche, although we might not realize what it is. Perhaps it stems from self-doubt, or negative talk sets in, but we all have more to offer than we care to admit or that we can identify within ourselves. Even when others tell us that we have a unique or needed skill, that we stand out for the work we do, that we should start a business or create a side hustle, the doubt still lingers.

We may convince ourselves that we do not have what it takes. We are not like the others. The keynote speakers, authors, podcasters, professional developers, consulting firms with their own LLCs and profitable businesses, who have their own brand. People who may have been labeled as "educelebrities", (a term that might not be popular) or referred to as "influencers." Educators who are in demand because of what they have written, a message they have shared, a niche that they fill—one unlike anyone else out there. But that is not us, right? It cannot be. We are just educators. Classroom teachers, administrators, tech coaches, paraprofessionals. The first step is to realize that we are not "just" anybody. We are individuals of impact.

How can we take it to the next level? How can we become edupreneurs? What do we have that makes us even come close to the edupreneurs who are out there, traveling, presenting, selling books, creating courses, delivering PD sessions, and working so much that being in the school daily is no longer an option? They have ascended to a new level. Educator with an idea, to entrepreneur with a movement. From entrepreneur to edupreneur. It is a demanding but highly rewarding business. How can we get there? Is it even possible? Yes.

You start with Dr. Will Deyamport. Educator, podcaster, innovator, and most importantly, friend and advocate for educators. I have known him for a few years, first as a guest on his podcast, the Dr. Will Show. I was honored to be invited because I did not believe that I had a story to tell. What could I possibly share that was unique, or would inspire, or that people would listen to? But it did not matter. You see, when you talk with Dr. Will, you realize that your voice matters. He hears you and is truly attentive to what you're saying. He leans in, listens, and helps push you in a direction to maximize your potential as an educator. Why?

Because of his passion for sharing your story and your words with those who need to hear and can learn from them. His zeal lies in helping you become an edupreneur, utilizing your talents to benefit others and realize your potential.

We have talent. We all have talents and sometimes, they may go unnoticed. Is it because we do not believe in ourselves, or think we aren't doing something special? Or is it because we lack opportunities to share our teacher talent with others? Only we know what we are capable of and where we can take it.

We observe others and their success. It seems so easy, right? It might seem that way, but it takes time, planning, failing, reflecting, and much more. It's a learning process like everything else. But it can be done. What do you want? For me, I want it all. I yearn for those moments in the classroom with my students. I want to learn from and work with edtech companies and organizations. I desire to use what I know about teaching and tech and blend them into my own business to make a difference for others. Giving up teaching wasn't an option. Taking on more was, because I know that I can make a difference, and I want to. So, I dove right in, and you can too.

Utilize your experiences, good or bad, to help others. That's where you begin. What do you wish someone had told you, showed you, helped you to understand? What guidance do you need? What are you doing in your classroom that is making a difference that others should know about? Consider the impact that you could make on others.

It's time to begin the transition from educator to entrepreneur to edupreneur. Is it easy? No, but it is absolutely worth it. We are modeling for our students the importance of building skills, of being adaptable, of sharing our knowledge and skills with others and explaining why that matters. It starts with us...the road to becoming an edupreneur awaits you.

My journey started when I recognized that we were doing some unique things in my classroom, and I began to share. Blogging came first, then conferences, then podcasts, then books, followed by my LLC. People were telling me that I was a connector. I could bridge teachers and tech companies together; I just "got it" and had a skill for facilitating these conversations and learning experiences. So, I dove in and so can you. I decided to start consulting, to create my LLC, to learn about the world of consulting, marketing, writing, and more.

It is challenging work, and it requires a constant pursuit of more. Utilize your talent, your strengths, and weaknesses, to build a business that helps you to grow and thrive. Maybe you will stay in the classroom, or perhaps it will lead you in another direction, equally impactful. You will recognize the value and understand that you are making a difference, even on the most difficult days.

Dr. Will has discovered his niche by becoming an edupreneur. Everything that Dr. Will has learned, he shares with you now. The questions you have will be answered. The uncertainties you harbor will be assuaged. And most importantly, the steps and inspiration that you need to become an edupreneur will be provided.

The choice is yours. Select your destiny. Discover what sets you apart, something that you can do or provide better than anyone else, develop your plan and simply begin. Most importantly, commence your path to becoming an edupreneur with Dr. Will today and enjoy the journey.

-Rachelle Dené Poth, J.D.

Now that we have adopted the mindset of putting actions behind our plans and venturing into entrepreneurship, let us focus on becoming that edupreneur.

Introduction

I define an edupreneur as a teacher/professor/educator who uses their knowledge base, skill set, and experiences to monetize their talents outside of the classroom. Though making an income is definitely a goal, the edupreneur seeks to tap into their *why* for becoming an educator to make a greater impact within the field of education. Like most educators, I didn't initially set out to become an edupreneur. I had no experience in business and never thought that this would be a journey I would embark upon. However, as fate would have it, I was at a conference, and I ran into an Assistant Superintendent of a neighboring school district who asked me if I often presented for other school districts. Later in the afternoon, he attended one of my sessions. I jokingly asked him if this was a job interview, and after my session, he told me he would be in touch. Two weeks later, he called to discuss what he wanted me to do. I subsequently sent over a proposal and an invoice, and that was my first introduction to educational consulting.

The funny thing was, once I received that first check in the mail, I was all in, but I still didn't have the experience, knowledge, or recipe to launch and run a profitable business successfully.

My enlightenment occurred years later, after I started researching more and pivoted my podcast to interview seasoned edupreneurs.

I wanted to write this book because there are educators contemplating monetizing their talents beyond their classroom but do not know where to start. Yes, there is no shortage of books on entrepreneurship or people you can follow on social media or YouTube. However, when you are an educator entering this arena, there is no definitive guide on how an educator should create an education-based business.

This book walks readers through the fundamentals of launching and scaling an education-based business. From learning about business formation, niching down, discovering your signature offer, social media marketing, personal branding, and much more, *The Edupreneur: Your Blueprint To Jumpstart And Scale Your Education Business* will teach you how to turn your calling into a business.

Being an edupreneur means cultivating a business mindset within the heart of an educator. The same energy we put into loving our students and creating lessons and activities must go into building a business.

I had so much to learn, and it has been a process of trial and error, along with the opportunity to interview many edupreneurs on my podcast. These edupreneurs are writing books, consulting, creating curriculum, selling lessons on Teachers Pay Teachers, leading masterminds, speaking, presenting at conferences, and coaching teachers in school districts with long-term well-paid contracts. Those conversations have been an invaluable education on learning how to be intentional with my business.

In this book, you'll find a combination of original content, complemented by quotes from conversations I had with five educators who were interviewed for my second documentary, *The Edupreneur: How to Launch An EDU Business*, which will be available later this summer. The contributing authors of this book are Dr. Tracy Timberlake, Jade Weatherington, Dr. Andrea Terrero Gabbadon, Valerie Lewis, and Chappel Billings.

Before you dive into the book, ask yourself: Why are you embarking on the journey of becoming an edupreneur?

What problem do you solve? How do you transform the lives of others with your product or service?

To whom would your product or service be most valuable?

Will Deyamport, III. Ed.D.

CHAPTER 1

THE CONVERSATION

"What happens if I were to live my life with no excuses?"

— JAY WILLIAMS

HOW DO YOU KNOW IF YOU'RE READY?

Some of us take the plunge because we want to make a greater impact outside of our roles within the school system. Others are drawn in from speaking at conferences, and some educators are yearning for a change. They need to feel reinvigorated and inspired and believe that becoming an edupreneur will bring back their swagger.

Becoming an edupreneur can be the right pivot, but it's not for everyone. If you're contemplating entering the field, there are a few questions to reflect on before taking the leap.

First, do you have a clear vision for the business idea you want to pursue? Just like having a set of standards and a pacing guide to steer you in a specific direction, starting a business requires directing a significant amount of time, energy, and resources toward accomplishing a specific goal. Additionally, it's essential to assess your risk tolerance and financial footing, as it can take time for a new business to become profitable.

Second, delve deeper into your skills and experience. Starting a business requires a diverse range of skills, including management, marketing, finance, and customer service. It's crucial to honestly assess your strengths and weaknesses and identify areas where you may need to develop new skills or seek support. Similarly, consider your classroom experiences and market fit. Starting a business in a new industry may be more challenging and require more research and learning than launching a business in a field where you have experience and connections.

Before writing this book, I interviewed Dr. Andrea T. Gabbadon, Shelly Terrell Sanchez, Valerie Lewis, Dr. Tracy Timberlake, Chappel Billings, and Jade Weatherington on this very topic of readiness. Chappel Billings, an Educational Consultant and Business Strategist encourages people thinking about transitioning into this space to "just start."

"We can get really caught up with trying to set up some kind of traditional shop, school, or institution. We think we have to have the front desk, the receptionist, the phone, the business cards, and the logo, among other things. The truth is, the only primary ingredient an entrepreneur needs is what's in the brain and the heart," she says.

"There will never be a perfect time to start your company, to launch that project, or to initiate that idea you've been sitting on for a long time. It is about learning how to just quite simply carry on saying what you say in the classroom, outside of the classroom. It is as simple as that."

"Be clear on what it is that you're teaching somebody. Your biggest challenge is going to be how to take what you do with your students everyday, whether it's young children, high schoolers, or in the university system, and learning how to change your language to apply it to your clients. More than anything, that switch of language is the most challenging part for an entrepreneur that is moving out of the traditional education system, because we are so used to calling people, pupils, or students. And now we simply have customers and clients."

Chappel encourages people to consider the following:

- Do I have the capacity? The physical, emotional, and economic capacity to launch something right now? Do I have the physical energy?
- Am I in a suitable place right now, either personally or with my family?
- Do I have the self-motivation at this point to put in 12-hour workdays and potentially not see the immediate results I would like?
- Am I willing to put in the work, understanding that, in the long term, I am ready to do what I need to succeed with this business idea?

Take some time to answer the questions.

One of the most significant lessons in edupreneurship is understanding where you fit in and whether there is a market for your product or service. You might have an impressive idea, a well-thought-out business model, and a polished product, but if you don't have customers for what you're selling, you have an expensive hobby, not a business.

Make sure to research who and what's trending in your space. Don't ignore the trends and pay attention to what school districts and conferences regularly invest in. Embrace the idea that this life will not mirror your life within a school district.

If you work in a school district or university, you know that as long as you show up, you'll receive a paycheck at the end of the month. As an edupreneur, it's up to you to ensure that check comes in, and to do that, you have to offer something your audience values.

According to Educational Consultant and Business Strategist Dr. Deana Stevenson, educators must do the following:

- Identify the skills you use in your current role as an educator that aid you in performing your job.
- Identify what problem those skills solve.
- Identify the transformation that occurs when the problem is solved.

I want to add another piece of the puzzle for you to consider:

- Identify the things you love to do that come to you as naturally as breathing.

Take some time to reflect, and jot down a few thoughts related to Dr. Deana's gems.

Chapter 2

Why People Buy What You Sell

"One of the hardest things in life to learn is which bridges to cross and which bridges to burn."

— Oprah

Niching Down: Owning What Makes You Different

Everyone has a unique set of skills and ways of thinking and being. Niching down is your chance to embrace this uniqueness and turn it into your greatest asset. What makes you different is what will set you apart. The journey of niching down involves self-awareness - identifying your strengths, understanding what resonates with you deeply, and aligning it with what the world needs.

A niche is more than just a specialized topic; it's a space where you are an authority, addressing a need of a specific audience. Think of it as "being a big fish in a small pond" rather than "a small fish in a big ocean." It's not about being a jack of all trades; it's about being a master of one. Whether you're a writer, a coach, a trainer, or a consultant, identifying your niche creates a connection between you and your audience. This allows you to break free from the mold.

The need to be different is a strategic necessity. In this landscape of Google Educators, MIEs, Apple Teachers, SEL folks and others, standing out is a non-negotiable. You have to differentiate yourself by offering something distinctive. When you're just another fish in the sea, it's easy to be overlooked. However, when you become the fish with human-like teeth that glows, attracting attention becomes inevitable.

Niching down doesn't mean limiting your potential; it's about focusing your efforts. When you focus on a narrower field, you have the opportunity to dive deeper and become an expert. It's the difference between knowing a little about a lot and knowing a lot about a little. Your expertise becomes a magnet, attracting those who seek specialized solutions. Clients, readers, or customers will turn to you because you're the trusted source in your niche.

Finding Your Niche: Carving Out a Specialized Path to Success

Let us go deeper into your niche and the problem you are solving. Everything you say, write, and create has to be a part of the framework or methodology you have developed to solve the one problem you have identified. You cannot confuse people by being everything or by trying to appeal to everyone. You have to be clear and concise on your *What* and the transformation your product or service provides.

Let me explain.

There is not an educator who has not heard about the need and the importance to identify their *Why*. And while understanding your motivation for doing the work is a great starting point and may get people excited in conference ballrooms, school districts do not pay for your *Why*, nor do people spend their money on your *Why*. Folks buy your book, school districts pay for your coaching or consulting services, and individuals buy your online courses or join your Masterminds because of your *What*.

Your *What* is your natural God-given talent(s). Your *What* is the best medium for sharing those talents (writing a book, a curriculum, creating a podcast, public speaking, coaching, teaching/training). Your *What* is how you connect with the audience who would most benefit from those talents.

Meet Shelly Sanchez Terrell: Author/Digital Innovator/International Speaker/Consultant/Teacher

Shelly Sanchez Terrell (@ShellTerrell) is an award-winning digital innovator, international speaker, and author of various education technology books. She has trained teachers in over 20 countries as a guest expert, consultant, and ambassador for the U.S. Embassy. She was named Woman of the Year by the National Association of Professional Women and received a Bammy Award as the founder of #Edchat. She has been recognized by several entities as a leader in the movement of teacher-driven professional development as the founder and organizer of various online conferences, Twitter chats, and webinars. She is the author of *TeacherRebootcamp.com, Hacking Digital Learning with Edtech Missions, The 30 Goals Challenge for Teachers*, and *Learning to Go: Integrating Mobile Learning in the Classroom*.

I spoke to Shelly about her journey in getting started as an edupreneur. Here is her backstory:

"At that time I was living in Germany, I had moved from school district teaching, and I was lonely. I did not know a lot of German. Within three months I had gotten married and moved there.

I started going online and thinking what are other ways I can connect and build a community. I started to take an online class to learn German, but then I saw other courses offered on other things.

Through connecting with people, I was asked to teach a class online.

I might as well try since I have a training background I can present on the live video, and they let you do it for free. So, I offered free courses at the beginning. And I decided, well, I love Twitter. And then I was growing so fast, and I thought okay, everybody wants to know how I am doing this and why I am so good at it. Within a month, I had five thousand followers which contributed to my enthusiasm. But I went ahead and did a Twitter for teachers or just Twitter in general.

That was my online monopoly because nobody was teaching on Twitter. I started getting all these people. I put my workbook out and then I had companies come and tell me, one of them I still work for till this day, say 'Wow you are a really great presenter. We want you to be our social media manager. We also want you to be our webinar host; it's free on Fridays. We are giving you your own platform.'

I looked at what some of the other ones were doing on their videos. They were doing the same thing. It was just a basic Power-Point, so for me it was more about figuring out how people want something genuine and real. When I applied that and went in an innovative approach that took off.

Then people started asking me to present live. Then I said OKAY well this is something I do not have to do for free anymore. This is something I should start figuring out on other platforms, other ways to be able to write a course. And so, I started really just writing courses, and presenting, and then books came later."

———

Shelly's story represents the moment we all have when we realize that we have something to say and something we need to share with a larger audience.

In building an education-focused business, the go-to is to look back at what you are doing well in your classroom or doing well leading a school. I get it. You want to start from a place of competence. But to play at this level, we all have to step outside our Zone of Excellence (the things we do well in our everyday lives as teachers) and step into our Zone of Genius (the thing we were born to do).

Your Zones

Genius		Excellence
The work you love that comes to you as naturally as breathing.		The work you do where you consistently receive positive reviews or feedback.
Incompetence		**Competence**
The work you do with consistent negative reviews or feedback.		The work you do well with little fulfillment or satisfaction.

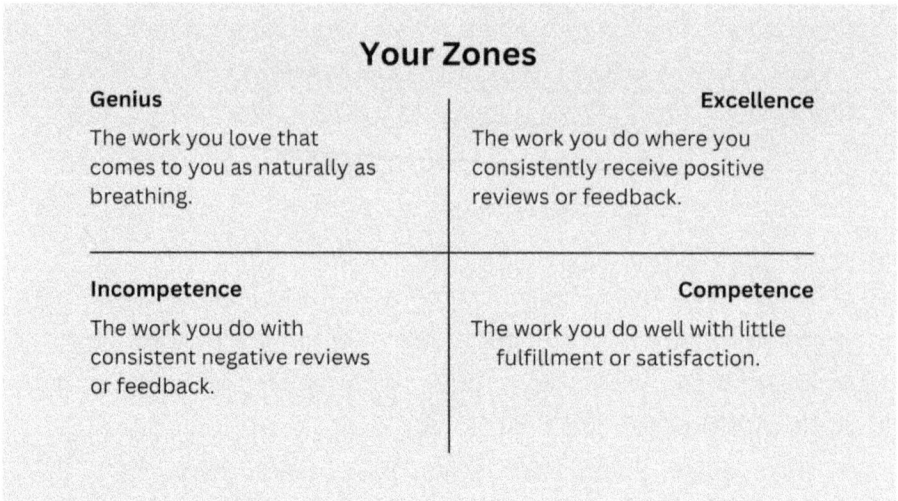

Your *What* is such a part of you that it can be easy to miss and thought of as something that is not special. But it is special and unique to you. Your *What* is about who you are and what fills you up. In niching down and solving a problem as an edupreneur, you have to discover how your *What* can serve others.

Have you identified your *What?* It is okay if you have not yet.

There are many assessments you can take to begin your journey in identifying your *What*. From the Myers-Briggs Personality Test to the StrengthsFinder Profile to the Enneagram, there are options available to guide you to find your *what* and how to use your *What* to meet the needs of your target audience.

In Steve Olsher's, book, *What Is Your What*, he does a great job in giving you the blueprint. In the book, Steve has what he calls the "What Equation." The What Equation makes it easier to identify your *what* so that you can begin your journey.

Think about the results from your assessment to complete the What Equation for yourself.

To _____ (action)
_____ (who) to _____(solution) by
leveraging _____ (your God-given talents) delivered via _____ (medium for sharing).

Think about your What Equation for a moment and let us jump into
getting clear on your offer.

Your goal is not to work with every teacher or school site. I know it is
tempting. I also know that you can feel like you are leaving money on the
table, but you are not here to build just a business for money or to be a
better version of so and so. You are here to build a business that not only
speaks to your soul, but also speaks to the right people.

———

*Meet Dr. Tracy Timberlake: Award Winning Business Coach,
Entrepreneur, and Influencer.*

Dr. Tracy Timberlake is a Multi-Award Winning Money
Mindset Business Coach, Speaker and Online Influencer. In the
last 7 years she has built not one, but two multi million dollar
businesses and teaches her clients to do the same by focusing on
methods that help them break out of the middle class money
mentality and elevating to a place of conscious wealth creation.

Recipient of the prestigious Miami 40 Under 40, she has spoken
on the TEDX stage, been featured on NBC, CBS, Entrepreneur
Magazine, etc.; it's no wonder her clients appropriately titled her,
"The Entrepreneur Whisperer." To date, over 15,000 people have
taken her online courses, workshops, and trainings.

I wanted to interview Dr. Tracy for this project because of a previous conversation we had for my podcast. Dr. Tracy is dynamic, captivating, and well-versed in business development.

In looking at our *What*, I asked her about her thoughts and this is what she had to say:

"I determined mine really by doing market research. When I first started in the online space, I came from a YouTuber background. I was a YouTube, beauty, and lifestyle blogger, and I really talked about my life and my hair and my makeup. And then when I started my online business.

I was helping people understand personal branding. And I tried to keep them separate, because my YouTube channel was very much hair, lip gloss makeup; it had nothing necessarily to do with personal branding. But then someone somewhere in a Facebook group found me on YouTube, and I said, oh my gosh, you have a YouTube channel. And at that point in time, I think I had over 1.5 million video views. I had maybe 15,000 subscribers at the time. And they wanted to know how did you do that?

I did not know that that was something that anybody wanted. Because I came from a YouTube background. And I thought everybody knew how to make a YouTube video. What do you mean, you do not know?

I did my own market research, popped into a few Facebook groups and started looking on Google on how to start a YouTube channel. I wanted to see how many people were Googling that and how many people were asking that question. Inside the Facebook groups, I got fifty responses in 15 minutes.

I knew that my very first digital product was going to be how to create a brand worthy video. It is called '*Nameless to Famous*'; it is one of my most popular ones. But that is how it began. I just did market research on what people were wanting."

———

SIGNATURE OFFER

Your signature offer is how you use your *What* to solve the problem and to serve your target audience. Sunny Lenarduzzi says, "You should only have one specific client at a specific place in their journey who is in need of a specific transformation."

Let us look at my What Equation: *To free teachers from being overwhelmed by a Learning Management System (LMS) by simplifying instruction and connecting teachers to what they do best via online webinars and in-person workshops.*

Knowing this is a great start but I still don't have a signature offer yet because I haven't identified an ideal client and the transformation my ideal client will undergo.

This is essential because everything your business puts out into the world has to concisely articulate what you do and how your customers will change after paying for your product or service.

Here's a look at my transformation statement:

I help CTE teachers who are struggling with the overwhelm of teaching with a Learning Management System to feel at ease, creative, and able to bring their best selves to their digital classroom.

Do you see what I did?

My statement speaks to a specific client, frustrated CTE teachers who are using an LMS. Those teachers are stressed and have anxiety from using an LMS in a blended learning, hybrid, or a completely online environment. And what I do with my training and coaching is to get teachers to feel at ease, tap into their creativity, and do what they already do best but within a digital space.

I took the information from my transformation statement and created a signature offer:

I offer LMS training, coaching, and on-going support for CTE teachers and CTE programs wanting to remove technology as an impediment to teachers becoming innovators in their classrooms by providing them with the tools, training, and support they need to meaningfully infuse technology into their classrooms.

Why is this important?

People do not pay for information; they have Google for that. They pay for transformation. That is where your business of solving one problem for one client becomes your differentiator. Remember you are not building a business to be better than so and so. You are the cheat code to solve their problem.

The biggest misconception about niching down is the idea or the feeling that you are going to be missing out on some business opportunities. Right?

One of the biggest problems edupreneurs can get wrong about niching down is not understanding that it is a process. It takes time for you to see it and for you to gradually own it. It is not something that you type in a Google Doc and say, yes, okay, this is my niche. Now, I am going to just do this. It does not happen that way.

In starting the process to define your niche, do not fall into the trap of positioning yourself as a better, cheaper version of XY and Z, over positioning yourself as different. This gives you and your clients clarity around what your business is and what it delivers. Rather than trying to be the next so and so in blended learning, *"be known for a niche that you can own."* - Christopher Lockhart and Heather Clancey

So how do you find your niche? You are going to start first with your expertise, your value, your vision, your message, and the kind of experience that you can offer to your potential customers. Now, look at your potential customers, their needs, their demands, their pain points, and what they are trying to achieve. Next, look at your delivery method or signature way of addressing the problem. Afterward, check out the areas where things begin to merge or overlap between your expertise and the customers' needs.

In mapping this out, you will begin to see what makes you different. Then you got to figure out how to deliver all that deliciousness to your customers the only way you can. Because at the end of the day, it is not so much about just selling a bunch of books or pushing your $99 offer and not worrying about what happened to them; it is about delivering on your promise to provide a solution to their problem.

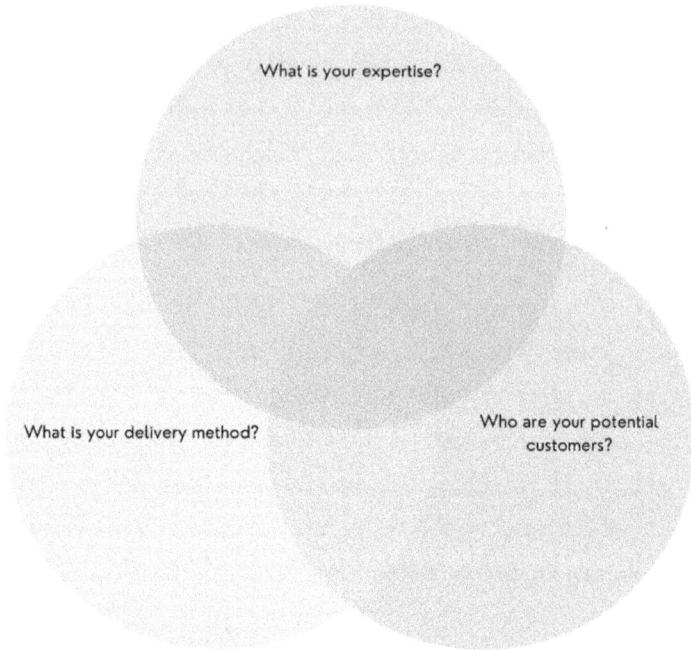

What is your expertise?

What is your delivery method?

Who are your potential customers?

What is your niche? What ideas do you have for signature offers? List them on the next page.

CHAPTER 3

THE FOUNDATION

"You're the only one that has a blueprint for yourself."

— DAYMOND JOHN

I started on these edupreneurial streets without registering my business and without any systems in place. I was winging it, reliant on a whim and a Google search. I was unaware of the importance of properly establishing a business and why I needed to create a business to do business. Before I understood the different options available for legally operating a business in my home state of Mississippi, I had been delivering professional development for school districts and organizations.

Dr. Andrea Gabbadon, Founder and CEO of ILM Consulting, learned that she had to register her business with the city and local school district. "I did not know that was a thing. However, I was able to tap into my professional network. There are other educational consultants that I know through my alumni group at the University of Pennsylvania, and they made recommendations," she said.

"I would also say some of these processes are rather nuanced, and so one thing that I hope surfaces is the importance of working in community and tapping into folks that have done this previously. Specifically, with logistics such as business registration, Employer Identification Number, and business insurance. I did not know anything about any of these concepts before launching into business."

Each city, state, and local school district will have their own policies in place. Be diligent in researching the paperwork, certifications, licenses, or other requirements needed to be eligible to work with school districts and universities. Don't put yourself in the position of having to turn down a job because you didn't have everything done on your end.

Registering your business means officially establishing it as a legal entity with the government. This involves completing the necessary paperwork and paying any required fees to obtain a business license, tax ID number, and other permits required for your specific business type and location.

There's nothing scary about the process. Generally, you can get this done online with one visit to your state's Secretary of State website.

There are several reasons why registering your business is necessary. First and foremost, it makes your business a legal entity, which means you can enter into contracts, sue and be sued, and own property in your business's name, thus protecting your personal assets in case of any legal issues that may arise.

Second, registering your business helps establish your credibility and professionalism. It shows potential customers, partners, and investors that you are serious about your business and willing to comply with regulations and laws.

Third, registering your business can provide tax benefits. Depending on the type of business entity you choose (such as a sole proprietorship, partnership, LLC, or corporation), you may be eligible for certain tax deductions or benefits.

Finally, registering your business is often a requirement to obtain financing from banks or other financial institutions. They may require proof of your business's legal standing before providing funding.

BUSINESS FORMATION: LEGAL AND STRUCTURAL CONSIDERATIONS

Starting a business involves several major steps such as identifying your target audience, defining your product/service, developing a marketing strategy, establishing systems routines, incorporating your business, purchasing domain names, and handling accounting and taxes. Incorporation is essential as it turns your business into a legal entity, properly structures it, and reduces legal risks, fines, and fees.

There are several types of business entities, each with its own pros and cons. The most common types include:

Sole Proprietorship is a type of business that is owned and operated by one individual and there is no legal distinction between the individual and the business:

- Advantages: Simple and easy to establish; the owner has total control, minimal regulatory requirements, and all profits go to the owner.
- Disadvantages: Due to the lack of separation between the owner and the business, the owner is responsible for all debts and is legally on the hook in case of litigation.

Partnership (General Partnership and Limited Partnership) is a business whereby an agreement is reached by two or more individuals who own and operate the business:

- Advantages: Easy to form, shared financial burden and management responsibilities, and potential for more diverse skills and resources.
- Disadvantages: General partners have unlimited personal liability, partners may have disagreements, and the business has a limited lifespan if one partner leaves.

Limited Liability Company (LLC) is a corporate structure that protects the owner(s) or investors from personal debt and liabilities of the company:

- Advantages: Owners (members) have limited liability, flexible management structure, pass-through taxation, and easier compliance compared to corporations.
- Disadvantages: Some states may make it more complex to form an LLC. There may be potential self-employment taxes, and the business has a limited lifespan if a member leaves or dies.

Corporation (C-Corporation and S-Corporation) is a legal structure where the owners or shareholders are taxed separately from the business:

- Advantages: Shareholders have limited liability, the business is a separate legal entity, it has a perpetual existence, ease of raising capital through stock issuance, and potential tax benefits for S-Corporations.
- Disadvantages: Complex formation and compliance, double taxation for C-Corporations (taxed at both corporate and individual levels), more regulatory requirements, and potential for disputes among shareholders.

Nonprofit Corporation is a legal entity created and operated with a focus on a social good and not with a focus on earning a profit. :

- Advantages: Exempt from federal income taxes and eligible for public and private grants, donations may be tax-deductible for donors, and directors and officers have limited liability.
- Disadvantages: There are strict restrictions on profit generation, specific reporting and compliance requirements, and limited activities outside the organization's mission.

An LLC is often the best choice as it provides personal liability protection. This means if your company is in debt or faces legal action, your personal assets such as your car, house, and investments are protected. Your business might go bankrupt, but your personal assets won't be at risk.

The choice of a business entity depends on factors like the size and nature of the business, liability concerns, tax implications, and long-term goals. It's crucial for entrepreneurs to carefully consider their specific needs and seek professional advice to select the most suitable structure for their business.

Before You Incorporate Your Business

Business Name: It's important to conduct a thorough research of your business name before settling on one. Choosing a name that's already in use can lead to considerable legal complications and expenses. To check the availability of a business name, you can use various sources:

- Your state's Secretary of State website.
- LLC Made Easy (https://llc-made-easy.com/free-llc-name-search-html), which takes you directly to your Secretary of State.
- Namechk (www.namechk.com).
- GoDaddy (www.godaddy.com).
- Google Domains (https://domains.google/).
- Namecheap (www.namecheap.com).

Valerie Lewis is regarded as an inspirational, skilled, and masterful educator. She is proud in tooting her own horn in sharing that "the art and science of teaching comes naturally" and her 23 years of experience in education and impacting lives of youth in and out of the classroom contribute to that. Her ability to design learning experiences around students' desires and interests is her superpower.

As a high school special education teacher of Language Arts and Fine Arts Academy Lead, she was recognized as the local school's Teacher of the Year (2016) in Gwinnett County, GA, where she then moved into the role of high school administrator.

We spoke over Zoom for the upcoming sequel to The Edupreneur documentary and this is what she had to say about building the foundation of her business, EdObstacles:

"So, for me, it was all a learning curve. I did not have the money to pay somebody to give me advice or to do it for me. So, I started off with going to my State Department's Secretary of State, and I did a search on fictitious names. I tried to think of something that would be a catchy name. I knew I wanted it to be with education. I knew that my business would have an obstacle course. So, I figure I would add obstacles to my search."

"I know I just created this name. But I had to be sure that nobody else had the same idea. I ran a search and if there were no matches that came up, I knew that I could go forward with the name I had chosen for my business. And right there on the State Department's Secretary of State's site, I registered my business name."

"For Georgia, it wasn't a hefty fee. If I remember correctly, it may have been around $100, maybe 150, to register the name of the business. Further, since I've got this obstacle course with kids running around, there is a likelihood of a kid falling down or injuring themselves. I knew I had no money. So, I needed to find the structure that was going to protect my personal assets from a lawsuit. And the structure I felt fit my need the most was to form an LLC or a Limited Liability Corporation."

"That way I knew they could not come directly for my assets, but it would still be official."

Please check with your state's Secretary of State to know what it costs to incorporate your business.

After ensuring that your chosen business name is available, make sure to buy the domain name for your business from one of the sources listed above. Once you've purchased your business domain name, create a professional email for that domain. For instance, if you've bought the domain for tdg.education, you'd be prompted to establish an email address for the domain.

Like Valerie, I initially went to the Secretary of State website for my state of Mississippi to register my first business. After a couple of years of non-movement, I closed my business.

A few years later, I was ready to once again step into these edupreneurial streets, but this time I used LegalZoom as a Registered Agent to incorporate my venture.

You can find registered agents in your state through a simple Google search. A registered agent can either be an individual or a business tasked with receiving and serving legal documents when your business is involved in legal actions such as a summons or a lawsuit. The registered agent will be your representative in court, not you. The registered agent will serve you papers, not the other party. Therefore, it's highly recommended to secure a registered agent rather than be the registered agent yourself unless you want to represent yourself in court. A popular registered agent is Northwest Registered Agent (https://www.northwestregisteredagent.com/).

A registered agent, also known as a statutory agent or agent for service of process, is assigned to receive crucial legal and official documents on behalf of a business entity. These documents generally include official state correspondence, tax notices, legal summons, and other compliance-related materials. The registered agent's address is where the state and other relevant authorities send these documents.

Here's why a budding entrepreneur might use a registered agent:

In some jurisdictions, having a registered agent is a legal requirement for business entities like corporations, limited liability companies (LLCs), and partnerships. The registered agent fulfills the mandatory requirement of having a physical address within the state where the business is registered.

The registered agent ensures the business remains compliant with state regulations by receiving and forwarding critical documents promptly. This arrangement ensures the business doesn't miss vital deadlines for filings, notices, or legal actions, which could lead to penalties or other negative consequences.

Using a registered agent allows business owners to keep their personal addresses off public record. Without a registered agent, business owners would need to use their own addresses, thus exposing them to potential unsolicited mail and privacy issues.

A registered agent must have a physical address within the state and be available during regular business hours to accept legal documents. For businesses operating in multiple states or with irregular office hours, using a registered agent ensures reliable document reception.

If a business plans to expand to other states or jurisdictions, having a registered agent in each state is necessary for compliance with local regulations.

Having a professional registered agent can enhance the professional image of the business, especially for those operating from a virtual office or a home-based business.

Overall, using a registered agent simplifies a business's administrative process, ensures compliance with legal requirements, and it allows you to focus on running your business confidently, knowing that important legal documents will be handled appropriately.

The upside to using a registered agent like LegalZoom is not having to worry about updating your information with your state Secretary of State's office. For a fee, they will submit the necessary paperwork for you.

BUILDING A STRONG FOUNDATION: THE ART OF BUSINESS DEVELOPMENT AND GROWTH

EIN: An Employer Identification Number (EIN) functions as the social security number for your business. You can apply for it with the IRS for free. This helps keep your personal and business identities separate. You should rarely use your personal social security number unless it's solely for verification purposes or you're comfortable using your SSN as a personal guarantee to secure business credit or funding. (www.irs.gov)

After registering your business with your state and obtaining an EIN, you can approach any bank or credit union to open a business account.

Bring your articles of incorporation and your EIN. The deposit amount depends on the specific bank or credit union. You can apply for most bank and credit accounts online. Some may require you to have a personal account before you can open a business bank account. Credit unions typically have lower interest rates and may require a specific personal credit score to open an account. The primary reason for opening a business account is to separate your personal funds from your business funds.

Don't forget to get a trademark for your business. Registering your business just protects your business name; it doesn't protect your brand name. For example, let's say your business is named PBIS. Registering your business allows you to legally conduct business under that name, but your brand is fair game. That is to say, someone else could also conduct business under the same name because you don't own the trademark for the name or any artwork/logo associated with it.

While you can apply for a trademark yourself, it's usually best to hire an expert or a trademark attorney to guide you through the process. One small measure you can take to protect your business is to add "TM" after your logo, which signals that you plan to trademark your business. You can also submit a trademark application that offers some protection until it's fully processed and approved. (www.uspto.gov/trademarks)

Business Licenses, Sales Tax, Sellers, and Permits: Most businesses need a sales tax and seller's license/permit, which authorizes them to sell products and services within their jurisdiction and collect taxes on sold products. When filing your taxes, you need to pay Uncle Sam his share. If your business requires a license or permit in your state, the best resource is the Secretary of State's online search engine. Fees vary, and the site can provide links for application processes.

———

*Meet Dr. Andrea Terrero Gabbadon: Founder and Executive
Director of ILM Consulting Group*

Dr. Andrea Terrero Gabbadon (she/her/ella) is a leadership
coach and the founder and lead principal of ILM
Consulting Group, LLC. Dr. Gabbadon's work touches on
culturally responsive and sustaining leadership, school organizational dynamics, and educator diversity. Previously, she
served as a high school teacher, teacher leader, instructional
coach, and assistant principal/director of curriculum and
instruction in both traditional public and charter schools.
Dr. Gabbadon has also served as an instructor of undergrad-
uate and graduate education, working with aspiring and in-
service teachers and school leaders at institutions such as
Temple University and Swarthmore College. She is a
frequent presenter at national conferences and has published
numerous articles in leading academic journals, evaluation
reports, and a book with ASCD entitled *Support and Retain
Educators of Color: 6 Principles for Culturally Affirming
Leadership.*

"When I first went into entrepreneurship, it was not a hasty decision. It was something I thought long and hard on and sought
the support of my own family to determine if it was the right
time for me to transition to this work. Are we in a good and
stable place in order for me to make the transition from working
full time with the benefits and all that includes? Am I actually
looking to leave my job for the right reasons or am I leaving on a
whim?

The answer to those questions and many others was yes. I also
discovered I had the bandwidth to launch full time and I started

tapping into potential customers, about six months before I actually started leaving my job.

My school district was well aware of my plans. They actually were some of my first clients. In fact, they were instrumental in giving me feedback on my business idea. I wanted to know if what I was willing to bring to the business world was actually a viable product that they needed.

Based upon their feedback, I knew that coaching was something that I was talented in. Coaching is also deeply connected to my why I love working with teachers and school leaders. I developed a record at my school with developing and coaching leaders as well as giving professional development. So, there was this proven track record of being good at this specific skill set.

It worked out well for me. They have made multiple referrals since and have been a repeat customer ever since. Having left, I also met with a wide range of entrepreneurs like technology enthusiasts, people in the medical industry, people from the nonprofit sector, and other educational consultants to share my ideas about what I am interested in doing.

For the first year, I used what's known as a Lean Canvas business model, which is simply a one-page business model. Every month, I revisited that model and made tweaks, like modifying my Unique Value Proposition or my target customers. The first year was essentially a trial period, allowing me to further refine the services I was offering, ensure relevancy, and address the gaps I identified in the industry.

That is ultimately what helped me understand that for school leaders, capacity is a huge issue in their urban setting and high quality materials are scarce and hard to find. These different strategies helped me not just identify what I was good at, but it helped me identify a group of people who needed my services."

———

The Lean Canvas Business Model

The Lean Canvas business model has emerged as a game-changing approach to business planning. Developed by serial entrepreneur Ash Maurya, the Lean Canvas offers a concise and dynamic framework for capturing and testing the fundamental elements of a business concept. Its streamlined nature and focus on rapid experimentation set it apart from traditional business plans, making it a favored choice among startups and established businesses alike.

Understanding the Lean Canvas

At its core, the Lean Canvas is a one-page visual representation of a business idea. It distills the key components of a business model into nine essential building blocks, each capturing a critical aspect of the venture. These components include:

- Defining the Problem: Articulate the specific pain points or challenges your target customers are facing.
- Addressing the Solution: Describe how your product or service solves the identified problems and provides value.
- Key Metrics: Determine the key performance indicators (KPIs) that will measure the success of your business.

- Unique Value Proposition (UVP): Clearly state what makes your offering unique and compelling to customers.
- Identify Channels: Outline the various channels through which you will reach and engage with your customers.
- Customer Segments: Define the distinct groups of customers you intend to serve.
- Revenue Streams: Identify the ways your business will generate revenue from your customers.
- Cost Structure: Detail the fixed and variable costs associated with running your business.
- Unfair Advantage: Highlight any distinctive factors that provide your business with a competitive edge.

Advantages of the Lean Canvas

The Lean Canvas model offers several distinct advantages over traditional business planning methods, contributing to its popularity and effectiveness in today's fast-paced business environment.

- A single-page format encourages clarity and brevity. This allows you to focus on core elements of your business so that you can prioritize and communicate your ideas more effectively.
- Embraces the principles of rapid iteration and agility. This allows you to quickly test assumptions, gather feedback, and make adjustments, facilitating a more responsive approach to business development.
- Encourages you to test your solutions to avoid investing time and resources into unproven concepts, leading to more informed decision-making.
- Places a strong focus on understanding and addressing customer needs.

- Is adaptable and can be tailored to work for various business sizes and industries.
- Visual nature of the Lean Canvas makes it an excellent communication tool. This allows you to communicate your business idea clearly to stakeholders, potential partners, and investors.

Lean Canvas vs. Traditional Business Plans

Compared to traditional lengthy business plans, the Lean Canvas offers a more dynamic and actionable alternative. Traditional plans often require extensive research, detailed financial projections, and comprehensive market analysis such as market size, market trends and opportunities, market demand and supply, and much more.

In contrast, the Lean Canvas encourages entrepreneurs to embrace uncertainty and take calculated risks. It prioritizes getting a minimum viable product (MVP) into the hands of customers as quickly as possible, allowing for rapid learning and refinement of the business concept. This is similar to you teaching a lesson for the first time with a tool you have never used before, and learning from the experience and making changes to the next lesson.

In this digital era, adaptability, speed, and innovation are paramount. The Lean Canvas presents a flexible approach to business planning. Its ability to assist you in getting to the essence of your business idea while fostering a culture of experimentation positions it as a powerful tool for entrepreneurs seeking to bring their visions to life in a marketplace that can change at any moment.

Please see a sample Lean Canvas below:

Sample Canvas Business Model

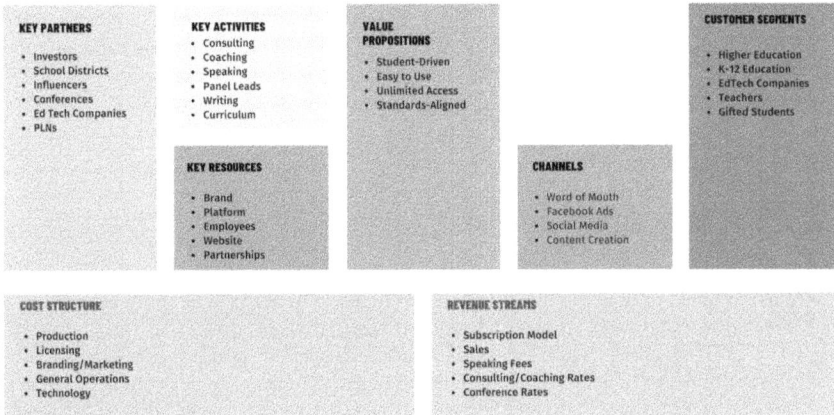

KEY PARTNERS	KEY ACTIVITIES	VALUE PROPOSITIONS		CUSTOMER SEGMENTS
• Investors • School Districts • Influencers • Conferences • Ed Tech Companies • PLNs	• Consulting • Coaching • Speaking • Panel Leads • Writing • Curriculum	• Student-Driven • Easy to Use • Unlimited Access • Standards-Aligned		• Higher Education • K-12 Education • EdTech Companies • Teachers • Gifted Students
	KEY RESOURCES • Brand • Platform • Employees • Website • Partnerships		**CHANNELS** • Word of Mouth • Facebook Ads • Social Media • Content Creation	

COST STRUCTURE	REVENUE STREAMS
• Production • Licensing • Branding/Marketing • General Operations • Technology	• Subscription Model • Sales • Speaking Fees • Consulting/Coaching Rates • Conference Rates

The Lean Canvas is a concise one-page strategic tool that entrepreneurs and businesses use to outline their key assumptions when developing a new business idea. It consists of the essential building blocks seen presented in the graphic above. By filling out each of these sections, the Lean Canvas helps businesses articulate their business model, test their assumptions, and iterate on their strategies efficiently. When applied to business platforms, the Lean Canvas becomes an important framework for platform selection, ensuring a clear understanding of your company's needs, while fostering adaptability and agility as the need to change arises.

Business Platforms and Setups

Business platforms are the foundational infrastructure upon which you will build and operate your business. These platforms encompass a range of digital tools, technologies, and systems that enable you to establish and grow your businesses in the digital age. Setting up these platforms involves understanding what you do and your deliverables and selecting and integrating various components such as websites, e-commerce systems, customer relationship management (CRM) software, and online marketing tools. This process aims to create an efficient ecosystem that facilitates product or service delivery, customer engagement, data analytics, and overall business operations. Putting together a series of systems in place allows you to effectively reach your target audience, streamline processes, analyze data for informed decision-making, and adapt to evolving market trends, and ultimately increase your chances of success in the competitive business landscape of edupreneurship.

You can implement a variety of services using these platforms:

Video Streaming Platforms:

- Zoom: An online video communications platform with an easy, reliable cloud platform for video and audio conferencing, chat, and webinars. https://zoom.us/
- Ecamm Live: A Mac software for HD live streaming, providing tools for broadcasting high-quality live video. https://www.ecam.com/

Online Course Platforms:

- Teachable: An all-in-one platform that helps you create and sell courses online. https://teachable.com/
- Thinkific: A software platform that enables entrepreneurs to create, market, sell, and deliver their own online courses. https://www.thinkific.com/
- Kajabi: An all-in-one business platform to create and scale your knowledge business. https://kajabi.com/

Training Platforms:

- Loom: A video messaging tool that helps you get your message across through instantly shareable videos. https://www.loom.com/
- Trainual: An online training manual for growing teams. It makes it easy to document every process, policy, and procedure in one place. https://trainual.com/

Scheduling Platforms:

- Calendly: An easy-to-use scheduling platform that allows clients to schedule appointments with you. https://calendly.com/
- Acuity Scheduling: An online assistant, working 24/7 to fill your schedule. https://www.acuityscheduling.com/
- JotForm: A full-featured online form builder that makes it easy to create robust forms and collect important data. https://www.jotform.com/

Additional Resources:

- Etsy: A global online marketplace, where people come together to make, sell, buy, and collect unique items. https://www.etsy.com/
- Fiverr: An online marketplace for freelance services. The company provides a platform for freelancers to offer services to customers worldwide. https://www.fiverr.com/
- Canva: A graphic design platform used to create social media graphics, presentations, posters, and other visual content. https://www.canva.com/
- Payhip: An e-commerce platform that enables anyone to sell digital products or memberships directly to their fans and followers. https://payhip.com/

Finally, don't forget to check if the website platform you're using to showcase your business incorporates several of the above features. It could save you money and time spent on research, and help cut expenses.

FINANCIAL MANAGEMENT PLATFORMS

When launching your business, you have to establish the types of payments and invoicing systems you'll use. One highly recommended platform is QuickBooks. QuickBooks is an accounting software suite created with the needs of small and medium-sized businesses in mind. It's easy to navigate, simple to learn, and designed intuitively. The platform offers a comprehensive set of tools for managing inventory, payroll, tax filing, accounts receivable and payable, invoicing, and general accounting.

Here are several other financial management platforms you might consider:

- ADP: A platform providing solutions for payroll, taxes, benefits, human resources, and compliance for businesses of all sizes. Visit the website at: https://www.adp.com/
- PayPal: An online payment system that supports online money transfers, serving as a digital alternative to traditional paper methods. Visit the website at: https://www.paypal.com/bizsignup/#/checkAccount
- Honeybook: A business management platform designed for solopreneurs and freelancers, which enables client management, project tracking, and invoicing. Visit the website at https://www.honeybook.com
- Stripe: A technology company that enables both individuals and businesses to accept payments over the internet. Visit the website at: https://stripe.com/
- Zoho: This platform offers a suite of online productivity tools and SaaS applications, including financial management tools. Visit the website at: https://www.zoho.com/
- Square: A financial services and mobile payment company that offers a range of business software, point-of-sale systems, and payment hardware products. Visit the website at: https://squareup.com/us/en
- Freshbooks: A cloud-based accounting solution that simplifies billing for small businesses, freelancers, and teams, making it easy, quick, and secure. Visit the website at: https://www.freshbooks.com/

To determine which of these platforms best fits your needs, it's advisable to assess the features each one offers. Always conduct thorough research and consult a financial professional before making a final decision.

MASTERING FINANCIAL SUCCESS: NAVIGATING THE MONEY CONVERSATION

As an edupreneur, securing a Certified Public Accountant (CPA) and attorney who comprehend the unique challenges and opportunities within the education sector can be instrumental for your business's success. Here's a guide to assist you in finding the right professionals:

Finding a Certified Public Accountant (CPA)

Look for CPAs with a background in working with edupreneurs, educational institutions, or similar businesses. They should have a solid understanding of the specific tax implications, accounting practices, and financial strategies relevant to the education industry.

Connect with fellow edupreneurs, educators, or business owners in the education field for recommendations. Referrals can be incredibly valuable when looking for a reliable and knowledgeable CPA.

Validate the CPA's credentials and certifications. Keep an eye out for any specializations they may have, such as tax planning for educational organizations or familiarity with educational grants and funding.

Arrange a meeting or phone call with potential CPAs to discuss your unique business needs and long-term goals. An efficient CPA will pay close attention to your specific circumstances and provide customized advice.

Communication is essential when working with any professional. Make sure the CPA can break down complex financial concepts into easily understandable language, even for those without a finance background.

In our tech-driven world, having a CPA who's adept with technology can streamline financial processes and enhance efficiency. Inquire about the accounting software and tools they utilize to manage client finances.

The CPA I use was referred to me by a colleague. I appreciate how Side By Side Tax Service, educated my wife and me on what qualifies as deductions, helping us make strategic investments in the business.

Finding an Attorney

Seek out an attorney who specializes in business or education law. Experience with educational regulations, contracts, intellectual property, and employment law will be advantageous.

As with finding a CPA, ask for referrals from other edupreneurs, educators, or business owners who have worked with attorneys in the education industry. Online reviews and testimonials can also offer valuable insights.

Schedule meetings with potential attorneys to discuss your business's legal needs, expansion plans, and other concerns. Evaluate their understanding of the education industry's nuances, Intellectual Property, and Trademarking.

Ask about the attorney's track record in handling cases or offering legal advice to edupreneurs. Success stories and case studies can help you evaluate their effectiveness in resolving similar issues. A good attorney should be responsive and accessible when you need their help. Ensure you feel comfortable communicating with them, and they are prompt in their responses.

Depending on your edupreneurial venture's scope, you might require an attorney familiar with both local and federal laws, especially if you're planning to expand beyond a single state or country.

Remember, finding the right CPA and attorney is a critical step in establishing a robust foundation for your edupreneurial journey. Invest the necessary time to research and interview potential professionals to ensure they possess the required expertise and understanding of the education industry to support your business's growth and compliance needs.

Protecting Your Business with Insurance

Needing to have business insurance can catch edupreneurs off guard. I know I didn't think about business insurance until I was awarded a gig with a university and had to fill out the Vendor Registration form to be approved as a new vendor. I checked off that I had insurance, but as soon as I submitted the form, I quickly called the insurance company I use for auto and home insurance and enrolled in a business insurance policy.

Depending on the services that you provide, your business might need a certain type of insurance that another business may not require. For example, if you are in technology or if you merely provide professional development to schools, you may only need one type of insurance. But if you work directly with kids in a school setting, you may need another type of insurance.

Dr. Gabbadon uses Hiscox for her coverage. She discovered Hiscox after speaking with clients and asking them about the specific insurance needed to work for their organization.

"That's when I found out that businesses do not just require general liability coverage and professional liability. But there are also specific insurances around working with students that I would be required to have, as well as insurance for materials and cars, because we do travel a lot from site to site."

Make sure you connect with an insurance professional and check with the entities you're interested in working with to determine which type of insurance you need. You want to be confident in knowing that you can not only be approved as a vendor but that your personal assets are protected.

Prior to joining my current school district, I was the Chief Social Strategist for Ingrid Stabb's company StrengthsFactors, which is now named StrengthsInNumbers. Ingrid is an edupreneur and became an approved vendor of the City of San Jose, after submitting an RFP. She did not need to purchase business insurance for a year, but when the city lawyers were ready to go into an actual Master Agreement between Ingrid's company and the city, at that point she called an insurance agent at XXX and purchased it for $50/month and showed the proof of insurance. At that point all the signers at the city signed the Master Agreement for over $300,000.

Personal Credit and Its Impact on Business Credit

Personal credit plays a major role in determining one's financial well-being and professional opportunities. Whether you're an individual seeking financial stability or an entrepreneur running a business, understanding personal credit and its impact on business credit is essential. This section will delve into the concept of personal credit, including what constitutes a good credit score, the factors that make up a credit score, and how personal credit influences business credit. Furthermore, we'll explore business credit and provide an in-depth breakdown of the Dun & Bradstreet (D&B) DUNS number.

Personal Credit 101: What is a Good Credit Score?

A credit score is a numerical representation of an individual's creditworthiness, indicating their ability to repay debts. Credit scores typically range from 300 to 850, with higher scores reflecting better creditworthiness. While different credit bureaus may use varying scoring models, a good credit score generally falls within the range of 670 to 850.

Components of a Credit Score: Several factors contribute to the calculation of a credit score. The most common components include: a) Payment History: The timeliness and consistency of bill payments. b) Credit Utilization: The proportion of available credit that an individual uses. c) Credit History Length: The length of time an individual has held credit accounts: a) Credit Mix: The variety of credit types an individual possesses (e.g., credit cards, loans). b) New Credit: Recent applications for new credit lines.

Personal Credit's Impact on Business Credit

Understanding the Connection: Although personal and business credit are separate, they are often intertwined, particularly for small business owners and entrepreneurs. When starting a business, lenders and suppliers may consider an individual's personal credit history when assessing creditworthiness due to the limited financial history of the business entity.

When seeking financing for a business, lenders may evaluate both personal and business credit scores. A strong personal credit history demonstrates responsible financial management and increases the likelihood of securing favorable loan terms. Conversely, poor personal credit may limit access to business loans or result in higher interest rates and more stringent repayment terms.

Protecting one's personal credit is vital for safeguarding business credit. Entrepreneurs should prioritize making timely payments, minimizing credit utilization, and monitoring their credit reports regularly. By doing so, they can position themselves favorably when seeking business financing or negotiating terms with suppliers.

Business Credit and the DUNS Number: What is Business Credit?

Business credit refers to a company's creditworthiness as assessed by credit bureaus and lenders. It reflects the financial history, payment patterns, and relationships a business has established with creditors and suppliers.

The DUNS number, developed by Dun & Bradstreet, is a unique identifier assigned to businesses worldwide. It serves as a universal identification system for businesses and is used extensively for credit reporting and evaluation. The DUNS number provides a standardized and reliable method for different entities to verify a company's legitimacy and creditworthiness.

The DUNS number is widely recognized and utilized by financial institutions, government agencies, and suppliers to evaluate a company's creditworthiness and establish business relationships. It enables businesses to build a credit profile, which can impact their ability to secure financing, win contracts, and negotiate favorable terms with suppliers.

The Different Credit Agencies

Credit agencies, also known as credit bureaus or credit reporting agencies, are organizations that collect and maintain credit information on individuals and businesses. They play a crucial role in the financial system by providing credit reports and credit scores that help lenders, businesses, and individuals assess creditworthiness and make informed financial decisions. Here, we'll explore the three major credit agencies: Equifax, Experian, and TransUnion.

Equifax is one of the largest credit reporting agencies globally and has a significant presence in North America. It gathers and maintains credit information on millions of consumers and businesses. Equifax provides credit reports and credit scores to individuals, lenders, and businesses, enabling them to evaluate credit risk and make lending decisions. The company also offers identity theft protection services and fraud prevention solutions.

Experian is another prominent credit reporting agency, operating in more than 37 countries. It collects and analyzes credit data on individuals and businesses to generate credit reports and credit scores. Experian's credit reports provide detailed information on an individual's credit history, payment patterns, outstanding debts, and public records. In addition to credit reporting services, Experian offers a wide range of analytics and marketing solutions to businesses.

TransUnion is a leading global credit agency that gathers credit information on consumers and businesses. It provides credit reports, credit scores, and other credit-related services to help individuals and businesses make informed financial decisions. TransUnion's credit reports include comprehensive information on credit accounts, payment history, and public records. The company also offers identity theft protection services and fraud management solutions.

It's important to note that while Equifax, Experian, and TransUnion are the three major credit reporting agencies, there are also smaller, specialized agencies that focus on specific sectors, such as business credit reporting or tenant screening. These specialized agencies provide valuable information to industries that require specific credit data beyond what the major credit agencies offer.

Credit agencies collect information from various sources, including lenders, financial institutions, public records, and other credit providers. They compile this information into credit reports, which summarize an individual or business's credit history and financial behavior. Credit scores, numerical representations of creditworthiness, are calculated based on the information within these reports.

Individuals have the right to request a free copy of their credit reports annually from each of the major credit agencies. Reviewing these reports regularly allows individuals to monitor their credit, identify any errors or discrepancies, and take steps to improve their credit standing if needed.

Here's a breakdown of credit score ranges and what constitutes a good credit score:

Excellent Credit: 800-850

- Individuals with credit scores in this range are considered to have excellent credit.
- They typically have a long credit history with a record of consistently on-time payments.
- They have a low credit utilization ratio, meaning they use a small portion of their available credit.
- Lenders generally view individuals in this range as highly creditworthy and offer them the best loan terms and interest rates.

Very Good Credit: 740-799

- Credit scores in this range are considered very good.
- Individuals in this range have a strong credit history and demonstrate responsible financial behavior.
- They have a good track record of making on-time payments.
- Lenders view individuals in this range as low-risk borrowers and are likely to offer them favorable terms.

Good Credit: 670-739

- A credit score in this range is considered good.
- Individuals in this range have a decent credit history and have demonstrated responsible credit management.
- They have a satisfactory payment record, but there may be occasional late payments.
- Lenders typically consider individuals in this range as moderate-risk borrowers and offer them reasonable loan terms.

Fair Credit: 580-669

- Credit scores in this range are considered fair.
- Individuals in this range may have a less-than-perfect credit history with some late payments or instances of delinquency.
- Lenders may view individuals in this range as higher-risk borrowers and may require additional documentation or charge higher interest rates.

Poor Credit: 300-579

- Credit scores in this range are considered poor.
- Individuals in this range have a history of significant credit problems, such as multiple late payments, defaults, or bankruptcies.
- Lenders consider individuals in this range as high-risk borrowers and may be hesitant to extend credit or offer less favorable terms.

It's important to note that credit score ranges may vary slightly depending on the credit scoring model used by different credit bureaus. However, the breakdown provided above gives a general idea of what is considered a good credit score.

Understanding personal credit and its influence on business credit is important for individuals and entrepreneurs alike. Maintaining a good personal credit score can significantly impact a business's ability to secure favorable financing terms and establish strong relationships with suppliers. Additionally, the DUNS number serves as an essential tool in building and managing business credit. By actively managing personal and business credit, individuals and entrepreneurs can pave the way for financial success and growth.

Developing a Healthy Money Mindset for Personal and Business Finances

Money mindset refers to an individual's beliefs, attitudes, and thoughts about money. It shapes our financial behavior and influences how we manage our personal and business finances. In this section, we will explore the concept of money mindset, its significance in personal and business finance management, and how our money scripts and familial experiences with money can impact our financial decisions and the success of our businesses.

Money mindset encompasses our deep-seated beliefs, values, and emotions related to money. It encompasses our attitudes towards earning, spending, saving, investing, and financial success. It involves our perceptions of abundance or scarcity, our confidence in handling money matters, and our overall relationship with wealth.

Having a healthy money mindset is vital for effective financial management. It influences our financial habits, decision-making processes, and our ability to create wealth. A positive money mindset empowers individuals to set and achieve financial goals, overcome challenges, and cultivate a healthy relationship with money.

Money Scripts and Familial Influences

Money scripts are the unconscious beliefs and stories we inherit or develop about money based on our experiences, upbringing, and societal influences. These scripts can be empowering or limiting and often shape our financial behavior without us realizing it. Examples of money scripts include beliefs like "money is the root of all evil" or "I'll never be wealthy."

Our familial experiences with money significantly influence our money mindset. The financial habits and attitudes we observed growing up can shape our perceptions of money and impact our financial decisions as adults. For instance, if we witnessed scarcity, financial stress, or unhealthy money management practices, we may internalize those beliefs and behaviors, affecting how we approach money in our personal and business lives.

My formative years were spent in struggle and doing without. Those years have left me to focus on security over risk and making saving money a priority over investing. I have such tunnel vision and such fear that I don't spend money on some things even when I have the money to do so.

If you've listened to my podcast, then you know that I have interviewed Financial Advisors, CPA's, and Financial Educators to talk about money in a real human way. As much as the interviews have been for my audience, they have been a start for me to heal my earlier financial wounds.

Cultivating Abundance and Growth Mindset

The first step in cultivating a healthy money mindset is to identify and challenge our limiting money scripts. By becoming aware of these beliefs and consciously reframing them, we can replace negative or restrictive scripts with empowering ones that support our financial goals and aspirations.

Adopting an abundance mindset involves focusing on opportunities, gratitude, and the belief that there is enough wealth to go around. A growth mindset encourages continuous learning, embracing challenges, and viewing failures as learning experiences. By cultivating these mindsets, educators can develop resilience, take calculated risks, and seek growth in their personal and business finances.

Developing a healthy money mindset requires ongoing education and support. Engaging in financial literacy programs, reading books on personal finance and entrepreneurship, and seeking guidance from mentors or financial professionals can provide valuable insights and strategies for improving one's financial well-being.

CHAPTER 4

HOW YOU BUILD IT SO THEY COME

"How many people you bless is how you measure success."

— RICK ROSS

EXPLORING PASSIONS AND SKILLS: UNCOVERING YOUR UNIQUE TALENTS AND INTERESTS

D r. Tracy is also Co-founder of Flourish Media and the Flourish Media Conference whose claim to fame is an annual event where they introduce women-owned businesses to potential investors for seed-funding of up to $15,000,000.

Dr. Tracy evangelizes that educators already come to table with a set of experiences and a skill set that are valuable in this digital age.

"Look at things like digital courses. That is a $300 billion industry with people who are making courses in the online space. And there are a variety of strategies that you can use to determine the skills that you have and your areas of expertise."

Ask your colleagues for feedback on the following:

- What are my strengths?
- What are my weaknesses?
- What do I enjoy doing in my current work?

"Start there and reflect on the times you've been praised at your school or school district. How can you potentially monetize that outside of that organization? You can also think about what are the things that are deeply connected to your why and how does this manifest in your day to day."

Think about the projects or initiatives you've led, the problems you've solved, and the impact you've made. Consider the feedback you've received from others and any awards or recognition you've received for your work.

Identify your gifts, or unique skills and talents. Consider what comes naturally to you, what you enjoy doing, and what sets you apart from others. This could be anything from a knack for storytelling to a deep understanding of educational technology.

Don't be afraid of your gift. "Your gift will make room for you." – Proverbs 18:16.

So for example, if SEL is your gift, and that's something that you have been asked to train other teachers in at your school, that is a sign of a direction to take.

The key is in understanding your gift and how it ties into your skill set and the work that comes to you as naturally as breathing. That self-awareness will give you the clarity you need to begin to discover your Unique Value Proposition.

Your value proposition should articulate what makes you different from other edupreneurs and what value you can bring to the education market.

To create a value proposition, start by identifying your target audience and the problem or challenge you are uniquely positioned to solve. Then, articulate how your skills, experience, and successes uniquely position you to solve this problem. Finally, explain how your solution will benefit your target audience, whether it's students, teachers, or school administrators.

FIGURING OUT YOUR CUSTOMERS' NEEDS: IMPLEMENTING THE ASK METHOD IN EDUCATION

The ASK Method is a powerful marketing and market research approach developed by Ryan Levesque. It revolves around the principle of asking targeted questions to better understand the specific needs and preferences of customers. By utilizing a series of carefully crafted surveys and quizzes, businesses can gain valuable insights into their audience's desires, pain points, and buying behavior. This information enables them to tailor their products, services, and marketing messages more effectively, resulting in higher engagement and conversion rates. The ASK Method's emphasis on customer feedback and data-driven decision-making has proven to be a game-changer for many companies, fostering stronger connections with their target market and driving sustainable business growth.

As edupreneurs, one of the fundamental aspects of designing meaningful products and delivering effective services is understanding what your clients need. Just because you can rock a crowd or know how to teach "50 ways to Google'ize your classroom," doesn't mean a school district or conference is going to come calling. The ASK Method can help you determine what your clients need and give you insight into their preferences, challenges, and goals, thereby allowing you to differentiate for the needs of your clients like you would for the students in your classroom.

Here's how you can implement The ASK Method in your business:

Conducting surveys and questionnaires is a straightforward yet effective way to gather information from potential clients. You can design surveys to collect feedback on areas of growth, experiences, methods of delivery, topics of interest, and areas where they need additional support. Open-ended questions can provide deeper insights into their thoughts and feelings, while multiple-choice questions can offer structured data for analysis.

Engaging in one-on-one interviews with decision-makers creates a conducive environment for them to express their opinions openly. For example, you can inquire about students outcomes, test data, district initiatives, and/or any specific challenges they face. These individual conversations can help build stronger relationships and build the know, like, and trust factor with those in a position to hire your company.

Utilize social media and online platforms to engage with your followers to better understand what's happening inside a multitude of classrooms and school districts around the country. You know this by being on Twitter and Facebook that educators often share their opinions, interests, and experiences on social media, giving you an additional channel for understanding their dreams and concerns.

By applying the ASK Method, you can make data-driven decisions about the direction of your company. Understanding what teachers and school districts actually want allows you to make business decisions on what you offer and develop relevant and engaging content.

Now let's get back to developing your Unique Value Proposition.

According to Harvard's iLabs, problems can fall into the following categories:

- Unworkable: This problem refers to a situation or condition that is not feasible, practical, or functional. It's a problem where the current approach or solution is not effective or efficient in achieving the desired goals. A value proposition targeting the unworkable problem would offer a solution that addresses the inherent flaws or limitations of the existing methods and provides a more viable and effective alternative.
- Unavoidable: This problem refers to challenges or issues that cannot be ignored or bypassed. These problems are an integral part of a situation or process and need to be dealt with in order to move forward. A value proposition focused on the unavoidable problem would offer a solution that directly addresses the critical issues that cannot be sidestepped.
- Urgent: This problem is one that demands immediate attention and action. It's a pressing concern that requires quick resolution to prevent negative consequences or to seize time-sensitive opportunities. A value proposition aimed at the urgent problem would provide a solution that can be implemented timely and efficiently.
- Underserved: This problem refers to a segment of the population or market that is not adequately addressed by existing products, services, or solutions. These individuals or groups have unique needs or preferences that are not being catered to. A value proposition targeting the underserved problem would offer a solution specifically tailored to meet the unmet needs of this neglected segment.

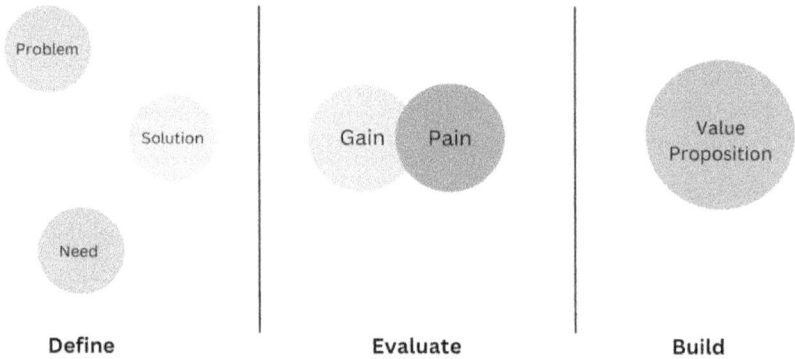

Your Value Proposition will ultimately address the following:

- For (*target audience*)
- Their dissatisfaction (*existing solution*)
- Due to (*specific unmet needs*)
- Your company offers (*product or service*)
- Provides (*key benefits of your solution*)

By taking the time to reflect on your clients' pain points, past experiences, successes, and gifts, and articulating a clear and compelling value proposition, you can separate yourself from other edupreneurs in the education market.

BRAINSTORMING SERVICES AND PRODUCTS TO SELL

Meet Chappel Billings: Educational Consultant and Business Strategist

With over 20 years of experience, Chappel Billings is a transformative leader dedicated to empowering learners through personalized, high-impact learning experiences enabled by technology. Chappel served in roles ranging from special education teacher to school administrator and instructional designer. After her tenure in the Greater Chicago educational landscape, Chappel served as a Teacher Excellence Initiative training facilitator and instructional designer at the Dallas Independent School District. Through her penchant for innovation, the team piloted the first principal recertification virtual course experience. Chappel also served as the Director of Digital Learning and Innovation at a Texas-based nonprofit, focusing on college and career-readiness e-learning products.

In our interview, Chappel shared her thoughts on the matter of brainstorming services stating, "I looked at the things that people kept coming to me for. Now I have two businesses. I had Chappel Billings Instructional Design, where I created online courses for organizations. I also had Dare To Launch, where I helped edupreneurs or aspiring entrepreneurs create the framework to launch their projects.

As I began developing online courses, people took notice and started approaching me with questions. They asked things like, "How did you create your course? What software do you use? Could you help me put together my own course?"

Sensing an opportunity, I started a small coaching program to help people launch online courses or projects. I contacted my first client directly after seeing her post on Facebook asking for help getting her course started. I outlined some initial ideas and let her know I could provide support in laying out a plan. From there, word-of-mouth spread as I worked with that first client, and soon more people were reaching out asking if I could help them launch their projects."

What I learned in our conversation is to not overthink this process. It's easy to go through everything we've done, everything we do, and create a long list of what skills of ours we could turn into a business.

Some options you have as an edupreneur to offer your audience are:

- Educational Consulting
- Offering Courses
- Keynote Speaking
- Becoming an Author

It is all about creating that *must-have* product or service. Creating should be fun and it should be something you feel people can really use and enjoy. Something that could make people's lives a little simpler or a little better.

Let us get into further detail on a few of the most known lanes available to you as an edupreneur.

EDUCATIONAL CONSULTING/COACHING/TRAINING

Education consultants are individuals who offer expert advice and guidance to schools, colleges, and other educational institutions on various aspects of education. They help organizations to improve their educational systems, processes, policies, and practices. The role of an educational consultant is an opportunity to pursue professional interests outside of the classroom and offer the opportunity to make a larger impact on the education system.

Education consultants typically possess a strong background in a specific area in education. They should also have several years of experience, either as teachers, administrators, coaches, instructional technologists, or researchers. To become an educational consultant, it is important to have a deep understanding of the education system, current education trends, and best practices.

This can't be stated enough. Your number one job as an educational consultant, coach, trainer, or author is delivering a transformation based on solving a specific problem.

Becoming an Educational Consultant

Start with your receipts! That's the expertise and experience that you already have from the years you have put in the work at a school or district, or edtech company.

Next, begin to create a tailored methodology or structured approach for organizing your training or workshops. This is paramount in ensuring a productive and impactful learning experience. Such a methodology provides a clear roadmap that guides both you and your participants through the learning process, fostering a sense of purpose and direction. This also serves the purpose of reminding your clients what makes you different, your value add.

Let me break it down for you...

Your methodology or secret recipe will define your objectives, outline content, and provide a sequencing of activities. This methodology will enable the seamless flow of information and skill acquisition. It also encompasses **how you do what you do**. It should be explicit in explaining how your sauce enhances engagement, knowledge retention, and leads to a specific transformation.

I know it's scary to jump out there. I have been in your shoes. The way to make the transition smoother is by building a network of contacts of other edupreneurs. Networking with educators, administrators, and other education professionals will help you establish yourself as an expert in the field and generate new business opportunities. You can also join professional organizations, such as ASCD, ISTE, or in my case, NCFR (National Council on Family Relations), to expand your network and connect with other educator entrepreneurs.

Don't sleep on recording your presentations, becoming guests on podcasts, and developing a portfolio that showcases your skills and expertise. Your portfolio should include examples of your work, such as sample lessons, research papers, presentations, and educational programs you have developed.

Offering Courses

Courses are an excellent option for edupreneurs. These courses can be delivered live, asynchronously online, or in-person and cover a wide range of topics, from academic subjects like math and science to more specialized areas like coaching, educational technology, and personal development.

There are several reasons why an educational consultant might offer courses. This includes providing additional value to clients, generating additional revenue, reaching a wider audience, and establishing themselves as a thought leader in their given niche.

The first step in launching an online course business is to conduct market research to determine if there is demand for the type of course you want to create. Look for online forums, social media groups, and other online communities where your potential customers may be discussing their needs. Next, start creating your course content, including video lectures, slides, quizzes, and any other materials that you will use to teach your students. Make sure that your content is organized in a logical and easy-to-follow manner.

There are several platforms you can use to host and sell your online course. Some popular options include Teachable, Thinkific, and Kajabi. Choose the platform that best meets your needs in terms of pricing, features, and ease of use.

While those platforms work great, you don't own them. As such, you need to create a website to promote your course and to serve as a hub for your business. You can use platforms like WordPress or Squarespace to create a professional-looking website even if you have no coding experience.

Start building an email list of potential customers who are interested in your course. Offer a lead magnet, such as a free ebook or video, to entice people to sign up for your list.

The elephant in the room is the pricing of your course. Some market-places like Coursera and Udemy will determine a price for your course for you, but for Teachable, Thinkific, and Kajabi, you have to figure out how much you will charge for your course by considering the value that your course provides and the prices of similar courses in your niche.

Finally, you want to launch your course. Some experienced in the game will advise you to use a Lead Magnet along with your email list to presell your course before your course is ready to go live. Some others go the route of marketing their course when they're ready to launch their course.

Whatever you decide, be sure to create a launch plan that includes promotional activities like webinars, email marketing, and social media marketing. Offer a special launch price or other incentives to encourage people to sign up for your course. And always collect feedback from your students and use it to improve your course. Do add additional modules or update existing content based on feedback you receive.

Public Speaking

Becoming a paid speaker can come with fame and the coin for those who have a talent for communication and the ability to engage with an audience. Whether you're looking to build a career as a keynote speaker, get in on motivational speaking, give TEDx talks, or become a lecturer, it starts with identifying your message and audience.

What are your core values and beliefs? What topics are you passionate about? Who do you want to connect with through your speaking engagements? Answering these questions will help you develop a clear message that resonates with your audience.

Now that is done, it's time to start working on your speaking and presentation skills. This can include things like practicing your posture, working on your breathing and vocal projection, and learning how to create a tight slide deck. Join a local Toastmasters club, take public speaking courses or workshops, and check out the YouTube Channels of some of your favorite speakers.

I know finding speaking engagements can be a challenge for new speakers. You can start by submitting proposals to local and regional conferences in your area. Reach out to event organizers and offer to speak at their events for free to gain experience and exposure. Attend industry events and meet other speakers who may be able to refer you to new opportunities.

Keep practicing and refining your skills to become the best public speaker you can be. Always remember to embrace who you really are, and to "take the person you see in the mirror every day with you." - Deon Cole.

It's worth mentioning because you don't want to get caught up in mimicking what other speakers are doing or trying to create a persona. That won't last and that won't sell either. You have to be yourself and only yourself if you want to truly connect with an audience. Stay away from the idea to "fake it til you make it." Make it til you make it. Never shy away from the work of self-awareness.

Don't forget to create a speaker reel that showcases your speaking skills and experience. It should include footage from your best speaking engagements and highlight your strengths as a speaker/storyteller. A great speaker reel can help you get booked for speaking engagements and increase your visibility in the industry.

Becoming an Author

We've watched the news come down our timeline on Twitter or Facebook and we've been to conferences where we've seen fellow educators share their book. With the existence of education publishers like EduMatch, Solution Tree, DBC Books, and Times 10 Publications, there are a lot more opportunities for educators to publish books and get them into the hands of other educators.

Start by researching publishers. Look for those that specialize in your niche or subject matter. Check out their submission guidelines and make sure your work fits their criteria.

Write a query letter: A query letter is a brief letter that introduces yourself and your work to the publisher. It should be concise and compelling, and include information such as the genre of your book, its word count, and a brief synopsis.

Follow the submission guidelines of the publisher and send your query letter and manuscript as instructed. Some publishers may require a sample chapter or a book proposal, so be prepared to provide these as well.

The publishing process can take time, so be prepared to wait several weeks or even months to hear back from publishers. If you don't hear back after a reasonable amount of time, you can follow up with the publisher to inquire about the status of your submission.

If you desire to go out alone, self-publishing has become an increasingly popular option for authors in recent years, and it can be a great way to get your work out to readers.

Either before or after you've written your book, you have to choose a publishing platform. There are several popular self-publishing platforms to choose from, such as Amazon Kindle Direct Publishing, Smashwords, and IngramSpark. Research the different platforms and choose the one that best suits your needs.

Your book needs to be formatted correctly for the publishing platform you choose. You can do this yourself using free tools like Kindle Create or Vellum, or you can hire a professional formatter.

Once your book is formatted and priced, upload it to your chosen publishing platform. Make sure to fill out all the necessary information, including a book description and keywords to help readers find your book.

Self-publishing means you will also be responsible for marketing your book. Creating a website or blog is an effective way to promote your book online. Use social media platforms like Twitter, Instagram, and Facebook to share information about your book and interact with potential readers.

Be sure to leverage book reviews. Give out a few copies to folks you know on social media and ask them to write a book review on Amazon and wherever your book is sold.

You can also provide a sample chapter or excerpt of your book on your website. This gives readers a taste of what to expect and can encourage them to buy the full book.

Additionally, attend book fairs, conferences, and other events where you can find opportunities to give readings, sign copies of your book, and participate in author panels.

Don't forget about your email list: Use your website or blog to collect email addresses from interested readers. Then, send out a regular newsletter to keep them updated on your book, speaking events, and other news.

Writing a book can be a great opportunity to promote yourself as a Thought Leader and an authority within your field. It's also the starting point to branch out into other lanes as an edupreneur like consulting, speaking, and offering courses, but it must be said that getting a book published is just the beginning.

The real work begins after the book is published. That's when you need to put in the work to turn your book into a business.

PRICING YOUR PRODUCTS AND SERVICES

First things first, know your worth. You're not just offering a service; you're transforming lives. Whether you're a consultant sharing invaluable insights, a speaker captivating audiences, or a coach guiding others to success, your expertise is the cheat code. Embrace that! Think about the countless hours, the sleepless nights, and the passion you've poured into your craft. Your price should reflect the value you bring to the table.

As an edupreneur, pricing your products and services can be a challenging task. You want to make sure that you are charging enough to cover your costs and make a profit while also being competitive in the market. The last thing you want is to be hitting the road on a weekly basis and barely breaking even.

So, how do you set a price tag that not only reflects your value but also attracts the right tribe of eager learners? Let's break it down, step by step.

Step 1: Determine Your Costs

The first step in pricing your products and services is to determine your costs. This includes both your fixed costs and your variable costs. Fixed costs are expenses that do not change, regardless of how much you sell, such as rent or salaries. Variable costs are expenses that vary with the amount of product or service you sell, such as materials or commission fees.

To calculate your costs, you should create a detailed list of all the expenses associated with producing and delivering your product or service. This list should include everything from the cost of materials to the time you spend creating and delivering your product or service.

Example: Let's say you are creating an online course. Your costs might include the cost of the platform you use to host the course, the cost of the device and/or any software you need to create the course content, and the time you spend creating and promoting the course.

Step 2: Determine Your Desired Profit Margin

The next step in pricing your products and services is to determine your desired profit margin. This is the amount of money you want to make on each sale after you have covered your costs. Your profit margin will depend on a number of factors, including the industry you are in and the level of competition in the market.

To determine your desired profit margin, you should first calculate your total costs. Once you have calculated your total costs, you can then add your desired profit margin to determine the total price you should charge for your product or service.

Example: Let's say your total costs for creating and delivering your online course are $1,000. You want to make a 50% profit on each sale, so you would add $500 to your total costs, bringing the total price you should charge for your course to $1,500.

Step 3: Research the Market

The next step in pricing your products and services is to research the market. This involves understanding your competitors and the prices they are charging for similar products or services. You should also consider the demand for your product or service and how much your target market is willing to pay for it.

To research the market, you can look at pricing information on competitor websites, talk to customers and other edupreneurs in your industry, and use online research tools to gather data on pricing trends in your industry.

For example, let's say you have researched the market and found that similar online courses in your industry are priced between $1,000 and $2,000. This information can help you determine where your product fits in the market and how much you should charge for it.

Step 4: Set Up Your Pricing Structure

The final step in pricing your products and services is to set up your pricing structure. There are several ways to structure your pricing, including flat pricing, tiered pricing, and dynamic pricing.

Flat pricing involves charging a set price for your product or service, regardless of the quantity or frequency of purchases. This is the simplest pricing structure and is often used for products or services with a low cost.

Tiered pricing involves offering different price points for different levels of service or product. This structure can be effective for products or services that have varying levels of complexity or features.

Dynamic pricing involves changing your pricing based on market demand or other factors, such as seasonality. This pricing structure can be effective for products or services that have a high level of competition or fluctuating demand.

For example, during the school year, demand for the service is high, and you may charge $100 per hour for tutoring sessions. However, during the summer months when students are on break, demand for the service drops, and you may have to adjust your pricing to attract more customers. You might lower your hourly rate to $75 per hour or offer discounts for multiple sessions booked at once. When adjusting your pricing based on demand, you are able to maximize revenue and attract more customers during slower periods.

Hopefully, you know a few edupreneurs in your circle. Reach out to them. Doing so is an invaluable way to gather information on pricing and what different entities are charging for their services. By leveraging your network, you can gain insights into a wide range of industries and fields. For example, within the speaking circuit, reaching out to fellow professionals can help you discover what conferences are offering as compensation to their speakers. Similarly, connecting with writers can shed light on what various websites are paying for articles, ensuring you have a better understanding of industry standards and negotiation potential. Expanding your reach to include district-level personnel and administrators can provide valuable information into what school districts are willing to pay for coaching services.

Lastly, tapping into the knowledge of individuals involved in the educational technology sector can help you gauge the rates that edtech companies are offering for contract work. This kind of networking with others and actively seeking information not only empowers you to make informed decisions about pricing but also fosters collaborative relationships that can lead to further professional growth and opportunities.

Whatever pricing structure you come up with, here are a few questions to ask yourself:

- How much do you want to make monthly or yearly in your business?
- What are you currently making in your business?
- How many customers are you serving each month or each year?
- What is the average dollar amount that a customer spends with you?

My old boss, Ingrid Stabb, MBA, coincidentally majored in Pricing Strategy at Yale. Her advice is to tie your pricing into how your solution solves your clients pain.

MAKING MONEY MOVES WITH RFP

Venturing into the Request for Proposal (RFP) process can be a strategic move for edupreneurs seeking sustained growth and expanded opportunities. By participating in the RFP process, you can position yourself to compete for and secure larger contracts, often with more established clients or government entities. This not only enhances revenue potential but also contributes to long-term stability. Successfully navigating the RFP landscape enables you to establish your business as a reliable partner, fostering trust and credibility within the industry. Moreover, winning RFPs opens the door to engagements beyond the one-and-done projects, as it establishes a precedent for ongoing partnerships. This continuity not only ensures a steady stream of work but also allows for the development of deeper, more collaborative relationships with clients, creating a foundation for sustained success and business expansion.

Request for Proposal Process

The Request for Proposal process is a common method used by school districts and universities to purchase goods and services from vendors. This process is designed to help ensure that the institution selects the best vendor to meet their needs, while also providing transparency and fairness to all interested parties. In this section, we will discuss the RFP process in detail, as well as provide tips and hacks for vendors looking to sell goods and services to school districts and universities.

Understanding the RFP Process

The RFP process typically begins with the institution issuing a Request for Proposal document to interested vendors. This document will typically include a description of the goods or services the institution is looking to purchase, as well as any requirements or specifications the vendor must meet. Vendors will then be given a set amount of time to submit a proposal in response to the RFP document.

Once the proposals have been submitted, the institution will typically form a committee to review them. This committee will evaluate each proposal based on a set of predetermined criteria, which may include factors such as cost, quality, and vendor experience. After the committee has reviewed all proposals, they will make a recommendation to the institution as to which vendor they believe is the best fit for their needs.

Tips for Vendors

If you are a vendor looking to sell goods or services to school districts or universities, there are several tips you can follow to increase your chances of success in the RFP process.

Before submitting a proposal, take the time to thoroughly understand the institution's needs and requirements. This will help you tailor your proposal to better meet their needs and increase your chances of being selected.

When submitting a proposal, make sure to be thorough and detail-oriented. Provide as much information as possible about your company, your products or services, and your experience. This will help the institution better understand what you have to offer and increase your chances of being selected.

While cost is certainly an important factor in the RFP process, it is not the only factor. Make sure to highlight the value you can provide to the institution, such as your expertise, quality of service, and ability to meet their specific needs.

Building relationships with key decision-makers at the institution can help increase your chances of being selected. Attend networking events, engage with them on social media, and try to establish a rapport with them.

Hacks for Vendors

In addition to these tips, there are several hacks that vendors can use to increase their chances of success in the RFP process.

Before submitting a proposal, do your research on the institution. Learn as much as you can about their needs, their decision-making process, and any past vendors they have worked with. This will help you tailor your proposal to better meet their needs and increase your chances of being selected.

Technology can be a powerful tool for vendors looking to sell goods and services to school districts and universities. Use social media to connect with decision-makers, leverage email marketing to keep them updated on your offerings, and use online project management tools to streamline the proposal process.

Instead of providing a one-size-fits-all solution, try to offer customized solutions that are tailored to the institution's unique needs. This will help you stand out from other vendors and increase your chances of being selected.

After submitting a proposal, make sure to follow up with the institution. Ask for feedback on your proposal, and try to address any concerns they may have. This will help keep your company top of mind and increase your chances of being selected.

CREATING INVOICES AND CONTRACTS

As an edupreneur, providing clear and professional documentation is essential for establishing trust and maintaining a successful business relationship with your clients. Two critical documents that facilitate this process are invoices and contracts. In this section, we will delve into the step-by-step process of creating these documents to ensure clarity, protection, and professionalism.

Section 1: Creating an Invoice

An invoice is a formal document that itemizes the products or services provided to a client and requests payment. It serves as a record of the transaction and outlines the terms of payment. Here's how to create an effective invoice:

Header Information:

- Your business name, address, and contact details.
- Invoice number (unique for each invoice).
- Invoice date (the date when the invoice is issued).

Client Details:

- Client's name, organization (if applicable), and contact information.

Description of Services or Products:

- Clearly list each service or product provided, along with a brief description and quantity (if applicable).

Itemized Costs:

- Include the unit cost and total cost for each service or product.
- Calculate the subtotal for all items.

Additional Charges:

- If applicable, include taxes, shipping costs, or any other additional charges.
- Clearly specify the details and rates for these charges.

Total Amount Due:

- Sum up the subtotal and additional charges to calculate the total amount due.

Payment Terms:

- Clearly state the payment due date and the accepted payment methods (e.g., bank transfer, check, credit card, etc.).
- Indicate any late payment penalties or discounts for early payment.

Additional Notes:

- Add any other relevant information, such as a thank-you message or instructions for payment.

Section 2: Creating a Contract

A contract is a legally binding agreement that outlines the terms and conditions of the business arrangement between you and your client. It is crucial to protect both parties' interests and ensure a clear understanding of the expectations. Here's a guide to creating a comprehensive contract:

Title and Introduction:

- Clearly state that the document is a contract.
- Include the names and contact details of both parties (your business and the client).

Scope of Work:

- Detail the services or products you will provide and the deliverables the client can expect.

Timeline:

- Specify the project's start date and the expected completion date or duration.

Payment Terms:

- Clearly outline the payment schedule, including any upfront deposits or milestone payments.
- Mention the currency and preferred payment methods.

Responsibilities and Obligations:

- Define the responsibilities of both parties to ensure a smooth collaboration.
- Specify any client obligations, such as providing necessary resources or information.

Intellectual Property:

- Address ownership and usage rights of any intellectual property created during the project.
- Clarify whether the client will have exclusive rights or if you retain some ownership.

Confidentiality:

- Include a confidentiality clause to protect sensitive information shared during the project.

Termination Clause:

- Outline the conditions under which either party can terminate the contract.
- Specify any notice period required before termination.

Dispute Resolution:

- Define how disputes will be handled, whether through mediation, arbitration, or legal proceedings.

Governing Law:

- Specify the jurisdiction and governing law that will apply to the contract. This means if there is arbitration or a lawsuit, which state will the legal proceedings take place.

Signatures:

- Leave space for both parties to sign and date the contract.
- Signatures indicate mutual acceptance and agreement to the terms.

Never slack in these two areas. Doing so can affect when and how you get paid. Creating clear and detailed expectations with your invoices and contracts sets you up for success. They also protect you in the event of any legal action. And always seek out the services of a lawyer for all legal matters related to your business. They can be useful in creating your contracts for you.

Remember to tailor each document to the specific project or client, and if needed, seek legal advice to ensure your documents comply with relevant laws and regulations. With solid invoices and contracts, you can confidently navigate business transactions and focus on the work of delivering transformative educational services and products.

BUILDING YOUR BRAND: UNLEASHING THE POWER OF PERSONAL IDENTITY

Your personal brand is the intentional expression of who you are, what you are, and what drives you. It's the deliberate curation of your authentic self, both online and offline, that sets you apart from the noise and leaves a lasting impression on others. Personal branding isn't about a logo or a color scheme or fancy cards and swag; it's about authentically showing up and showcasing your expertise, passions, and values to attract your people, whether it's potential clients, partnerships, or a community. When you harness the power of your personal brand, you position yourself as an authority in your niche, build trust, and open doors to the *right* opportunities.

Don't think of branding as a way to market yourself as the next so and so. That won't work and you're not going to be successful if you're not willing to unapologetically be yourself and not give a *@%^ about what others think about the *real* you.

Along the way, you may lose friends, followers, clients, and other opportunities. That may be jarring to hear, but it's okay not to be liked for being who you are because authenticity should never be compromised to seek approval from others.

Bringing everything to the table that makes you who you are is the power of your personal brand.

———————

Meet Dr. Will Deyamport, III: Entrepreneurial Thinker, LMS Jedi, and Podcaster

I fell into edtech via divine intervention. I never planned for this career and never thought I would be where I am now. After graduating from The University of Southern Mississippi with a degree in Radio, TV, and Film, I headed to Boston where I worked for UMASS Boston, leading a college and career mentoring program for their GEARUP grant. I worked with 6th and 7th graders, and my job consisted of organizing college visits, bringing in guest speakers, and creating career-mentoring focused events.

Three years later, I left Boston and returned to Mississippi to pursue another Bachelor's degree in Child and Family Studies with an emphasis in Family Relations. I did so because I had planned to continue to work in youth development and wanted a foundational knowledge to take me to the next level. In 2004, I graduated and decided to apply to graduate school to fill in my gaps in educational philosophy, curriculum and instruction, classroom management, classroom assessment, coaching, and life and career development. I was well on my way to building up my toolkit to pursue higher-level leadership roles in youth-serving entities.

Between interviewing for jobs, launching a failed business, and working as the Chief Social Strategist for StrengthsFactors, now Strengths In Numbers, I became intrigued with working in higher education. After speaking with a group of Student Affairs professionals and conducting several informational interviews, I made the decision to pursue a doctoral degree in Educational Leadership and Management at Capella University.

Along the way, I began to present at conferences on the uses of technology in the classroom. I made a name for myself and met a bunch of folks on Twitter who would shape the trajectory of my career. Before graduating with my Ed.D., I was offered a full-time position as a District Instructional Technologist in the summer of 2013.

As my presence and influence grew on Twitter, I continued presenting and leading workshops wherever I could. I also started writing blog posts and articles for publications such as TechEdge magazine, District Administration, and Schoology Exchange. Additionally, I launched a podcast that focused on all things edtech. That momentum and recognition led to my first consulting gig, delivering Google training for CTE teachers for a school district in Mississippi.

Over the past 11 years, my interests have changed. I no longer want to be brought in to "fix" the issue of teachers not using the tech the district has purchased. I also don't want to be in the business of changing teachers' minds about going digital. Fixing is exhausting and I just don't have the bandwidth anymore.

If you know me via Twitter, then you know that I took a different direction for my podcast five years ago. That pivot birthed The Edupreneur documentary and a whole new outlook on education. I believe that entrepreneurial thinking can not only be used to create the kind of teaching practices that reach this mobile generation of learners, but can also unleash the best within educators, encouraging them to take ownership over their lives and careers by thinking of themselves a business of one.

————

My Branding Story

When I started my journey to building my personal brand, I didn't have a clear understanding of what my personal brand would be. I knew I wanted to work in education, but I wasn't sure how or in what capacity. Do I stay focused on edtech, or do I pivot and go all in with financial literacy and entrepreneurship education? Hence this book you're reading.

It wasn't until I took the time to reflect on my values, passions, and goals that I was able to find my personal brand.

One of the first steps I took was to identify my values. I asked myself, what is most important to me? I came up with a list of values that included ownership, creativity, financial freedom, and helping others find those things for themselves. Once I had a clear understanding of my values, I was able to use them as a foundation for my personal brand.

Next, I thought about my passions. What topics did I enjoy talking about? What did I enjoy doing? I loved podcasting, learning, and talking about education being more than rote memorization and financial literacy and entrepreneurship, so I decided to build my personal brand around that. I wanted to help educators to take on an entrepreneurial mindset, to bring entrepreneurial thinking into their teaching. I also wanted educators to monetize their talents beyond the walls of their classrooms and to get their financial houses in order, just like I was building mine.

Finally, I thought about my purpose. What was my why? Why did I want to build a personal brand? I realized that I wanted to help educators to define and create their best lives. I wanted them to be unashamed to be their best selves and reach their fullest potential.

By combining my values, passions, and purpose, I was able to find my personal brand. I pivoted my podcast, created a documentary, and started to present on content at conferences that was consistent with my values. I took every opportunity to share my message with others. I used social media platforms like Twitter, Facebook, and LinkedIn to build my brand, and I made sure to stay authentic and true to myself, even after seeing relationships and connections with folks disappear.

Over time, my personal brand evolved, but the foundation remained the same. I continue to focus on helping educators become unrestrained from the shackles of traditional teaching and anchored in evangelizing the need for educators to take control over their careers. I have built a community of like-minded individuals who share my values, and I try to use my voice to make an impact in the world.

Developing A Personal Brand

Developing a memorable personal brand is a significant aspect of success in today's competitive world. This is particularly true for edupreneurs who combine their passion for education with entrepreneurial skills to create and develop transformational educational products, services, or solutions.

Why is personal branding important for edupreneurs?

As an edupreneur, you are not just selling a product or service, but your expertise and knowledge. Your personal brand (your different) is what sets you apart from the competition and establishes your credibility as a *thought leader* in your field. A strong personal brand can help you:

Build trust and establish credibility: Sharing your knowledge and expertise can establish yourself as an authority in your niche, and gain the trust of your audience.

Attract and retain customers: A strong personal brand can help you attract new customers and retain existing ones by creating an emotional connection with them. People are more likely to do business with someone *they know, like, and trust.*

Differentiate yourself from the competition: With so many edupreneurs vying for attention, a strong personal brand can help you stand out from the competition. It can also help you charge a premium for your services.

How to develop your personal brand as an edupreneur?

To build a strong personal brand, you need to know who you are speaking to, define your niche and target audience, and know what problems you are trying to solve. Additionally, you must be consistent in creating content that speaks directly to your target audience.

Your personal brand should reflect who you are as a person and what you stand for. Embrace everything that makes you who you are, and let that shine through in your content.

To establish yourself as an authority in your niche, you need to create valuable content that provides solutions to your audience's problems. This can include blog posts, podcasts, videos, social media posts, IG Reels, and more.

Building relationships with other edupreneurs can help you expand your reach and grow your personal brand. Attend conferences, join online groups, and collaborate on projects with other experts in your niche.

Your online presence is often the first impression people will have of your personal brand. Create a professional website, optimize your social media profiles, and consistently post relevant content to build your online presence.

The spirit of your personal brand should be at the heart and soul of what you communicate to the world. It's the message you want to convey and the values you want to stand for. Your personal brand should be a reflection of your personality, your passion, and your purpose. It's about being true to yourself and staying authentic to your beliefs, even if you turn off some folks in the process.

Being authentically yourself and being different means understanding you aren't the only educator speaking, writing, presenting, and/or coaching and training on your subject matter. As such, standing out and separating yourself from the educator who is delivering products and services within your area is necessary to get your name into the hearts and minds of potential clients and fans alike. Don't be afraid to put yourself out there and let who you really are shine.

Remember, personal branding is a long-term investment, and it takes time and effort to build a brand that truly represents who you are and what you stand for.

Marketing And Building An Audience

Marketing plays an important role in attracting customers. To market a product or service requires you to build a community and pinpoint your target audience.

Building a community takes an in-depth understanding of your business and what it offers. One way to do this is to create content that shares how your product or service provides value. This can include blog posts, videos, social media content, and other types of media that connect with your community.

Another way to build a community is to engage with potential customers through social media platforms. You can use these platforms to interact with customers, answer their questions, and share valuable information about your product or service. This can help you build a relationship with your audience and establish trust and credibility.

Once you have built a community, the next step is to pinpoint your target audience. This requires a deep understanding of your product or service and the problem it solves. You need to identify the characteristics of your ideal customer, including their demographics, interests, and behavior.

One way to pinpoint your target audience is to conduct market research. This can include surveys, focus groups, webinars, and livestreams. You can also use informal interviews to identify patterns and gaps in the market.

You can also identify your target audience by creating a customer avatar or buyer persona. A buyer persona is a fictional representation of your ideal customer, based on real-world data and insights. This can help you understand your target audience better and create marketing strategies that resonate with them.

Content Marketing for Your Business

Content marketing is the use of free content and social media to market your business products and/or service. It provides a way for you to engage with customers existing or new. For content marketing as an edupreneur you should identify and set your goals (purpose/why), choose which social media platform you would like to use (to create a strong profile), start a content calendar (to automate your postings), be social (engage with your audience), build your following (paid campaigns), and take in leads (followers who seem to be interested).

———

Meet Jade Weatherington: Online Teacher, Course Creator, and Business Strategist

Dubbed *"The Six-Figrue Teacher" in Forbes and Business Insider,* Jade Weatherington started teaching online in 2008 as a side hustle but turned the hustle into a lucrative business. She is the owner and founder of Teacher Jade's Writing Academy which is an online school providing writing assistance to youth ages 8-18. She also teaches others how to develop and sell online courses. To learn more about, check out www.TeacherJade.com

The following are a few gems from Jade:
"Educators, who are also entrepreneurs, can benefit from providing free content to offer a preview of the value that potential customers can expect from their products. For example, if you are a classroom teacher, you probably have stacks of lesson plans. Each lesson plan can be sold on platforms like TPT or even your own website. But, why would someone buy your lesson plans if they don't know anything about your teaching style? Well, you provide them with ONE free lesson plan, make social media content of yourself teaching that lesson, and if they like what they see, they're more inclined to purchase the other lesson plans. I have multi mini courses that are free. They don't take much time to create, but I can leverage insights from the content to determine what courses I should make next. And, those are the courses I put a price tag on. The free content acts as a teaser, allowing potential clients to experience the quality and expertise I can offer before they make a commitment to purchase. In addition to them signing up for a free course, I can add them to my newsletter to further entice

them to purchase a course later on. It's all about creating the sales funnel.

Not only do I provide free content, but I utilize free publicity. Drawing attention to my brand is important and one way I do this is through interviews. When people read about my experience, they will then come to my website where I have my free offerings. They can also find me on social media. Now, my approach to social media does not follow the typical strategies. I used to post consistently. However, based on my own website insights, that was not where I was drawing my biggest audience, so I greatly reduced my postings and focused on building my email list.

However, for those of you that are just starting out, post often. You have to engage with your audience, or they won't know who you are. Track your insights to see what is working versus what isn't working. When you make an offer, provide a sneak peek or something of interest to further engage your audience. Eventually, the free labor that you have invested will become the income that you wanted!"

———

Content marketing is a strategic approach to creating and distributing valuable, relevant, and consistent content to attract and engage a target audience. In an era where digital presence is paramount, you can leverage content marketing to build brand awareness, establish authority, and drive customer loyalty. As part of this strategy, the following tools play a crucial role in optimizing and organizing content dissemination:

- Linktree: https://linktr.ee/
- Facebook: https://www.facebook.com/
- Instagram: https://www/.instagram,com/
- Twitter: https://www.twitter.com/
- TikTok: https://www.tiktok.com/en/
- Pinterest: https://www.pinterest.com/

Linktree is a popular link management tool that allows users, especially content creators and businesses, to create a single link that houses multiple links to their various online platforms. This way, you can easily direct your followers to different destinations such as websites, social media profiles, online stores, and more, through one unified link.

Facebook is one of the world's largest and most popular social media platforms. It enables users to connect and interact with friends, family, and acquaintances through posts, messages, and multimedia sharing. Users can join or create groups, follow pages of their interests, and engage in various activities, making it a versatile platform for personal connections, social networking, and business marketing and promotion.

Instagram is a visually fueled social media platform known for its emphasis on sharing photos and short videos. It allows users to follow others, like and comment on posts, and use hashtags to discover content of their interest. It's widely used by individuals, influencers, brands, and businesses to connect with their customers and promote their products or services.

Twitter (X) is a microblogging platform where users can share short messages known as tweets (up to 280 characters). It is designed for real-time conversations, news updates, and sharing thoughts or opinions. On Twitter (X), you can find breaking news, trending topics, and discussions on various subjects. Users can follow each other to receive updates from people or organizations of their interest.

TikTok is a video-sharing social media platform that is immensely popular, especially among younger audiences. Users can create and share short videos set to music. The platform's focus on short-form video has made it a captivating and engaging platform for entertainment and content discovery.

Pinterest is a visual discovery and bookmarking platform that allows users to create and curate collections of images and videos known as "pins." Users can organize pins into thematic boards, serving as virtual inspiration boards for various interests and projects. Pinterest is commonly used for discovering ideas, recipes, DIY projects, fashion inspiration, and more, making it a valuable platform for curating content.

Hootsuite is a social media platform that allows you to pre-plan your social media posting across the following channels: X (Formerly Twitter), Facebook, Instagram, LinkedIn, and YouTube.

Repurpose all material for every social media platform that you use. Also, the wonderful thing about all these platforms is that they can all be managed from one or two systems.

Content Marketing Is for Thought Leadership

Thought leadership is a powerful concept that holds immense value for edupreneurs, particularly those who engage in speaking engagements and authorship. It goes beyond simply sharing knowledge and insights; it is about cultivating a distinct perspective and actively shaping the narrative in your respective field. By establishing yourself as a thought leader, you can gain credibility, build influence, and make a lasting impact with your audience.

At its core, thought leadership is about being at the forefront of knowledge and innovation within a specific domain. Edupreneurs who embody this role are not only experts in their field but also have a deep understanding of emerging trends, challenges, and opportunities. By constantly staying abreast of developments and conducting research, they possess a unique ability to synthesize complex information and distill it into accessible and meaningful insights. This expertise empowers them to provide valuable guidance and offer fresh perspectives to their audience.

The importance of thought leadership for you, especially as a speaker or an author, cannot be overstated. As a speaker, you have the opportunity to deliver compelling presentations, captivating audiences with your ideas and vision. Being recognized as a thought leader commands attention, and your words carry weight and influence. Your expertise and insights become a magnet, attracting event organizers and participants, enabling you to secure speaking engagements at conferences, seminars, and workshops.

Similarly, as authors, thought leaders have the power to shape the discourse in their field through the written word. Sharing your knowledge and experiences in books, articles, and whitepapers leaves a lasting legacy. Readers seek out your publications, eager to gain insights, acquire new skills, and be inspired by your perspectives. Thought leaders can spark conversations, challenge existing paradigms, and propose innovative solutions, making a profound impact on their readers and the larger educational community.

Moreover, thought leadership opens doors to collaborations and partnerships. As recognized authorities in their field, edupreneurs are often approached by like-minded individuals and organizations for joint ventures, research projects, and consulting opportunities. These collaborations not only enhance their visibility and reach but also allow them to exchange ideas and learn from other thought leaders, fostering a culture of continuous growth and development.

Furthermore, thought leadership serves as a foundation for building a personal brand. By consistently delivering high-quality content and sharing valuable insights, you can establish yourself as a go-to expert in your niche. This reputation amplifies your credibility, which, in turn, attracts opportunities for media appearances, interviews, and guest contributions to industry publications. The visibility gained through these channels further solidifies your position as an influential figure in the educational landscape.

In creating your content, who owns it? Is it you? Is it the book publisher? The conference? Or the website or the magazine?

To own one's IP means to have legal ownership and control over one's intellectual property (IP). Intellectual property refers to creations of the mind, such as inventions, literary and artistic works, and symbols, names, and images used in commerce. Owning one's IP means that the individual or entity has the exclusive rights to use, reproduce, distribute, and license their intellectual creations.

INTELLECTUAL PROPERTY AND EDUCATORS' OWNERSHIP

In today's digital age, intellectual property (IP) has become a critical concern for individuals in various creative fields. Educators, in particular, play a key role in generating educational content and developing innovative teaching strategies. However, the question of who owns the intellectual property rights to educational materials created by educators has been a topic of debate. This section explores the importance of educators owning what they create and the need for them to purchase their own tablets and laptops to safeguard their intellectual property rights.

There are several forms of intellectual property, and ownership can vary depending on the type:

Copyright is related to the creation of original literary, artistic, or musical works (e.g., books, songs, paintings); you automatically own the copyright to those works. This means you have the exclusive right to reproduce, distribute, and display your creations. You can also license or sell these rights to others. That said, in the case of a book, the publisher can own the copyright if an agreement is made between the company and the author.

Trademarks protect symbols, names, and slogans used to identify goods and services in commerce. Owning a trademark means you have exclusive rights to use that mark in connection with your products or services, and you can prevent others from using it without permission.

Patents grant inventors exclusive rights to their inventions for a set period, usually 20 years. Owning a patent means you can prevent others from making, using, selling, or importing your patented invention without your permission.

Trade Secrets are valuable business information, like formulas, manufacturing processes, or customer lists, that provide a competitive advantage. Owning trade secrets means keeping this information confidential and taking legal action if someone misappropriates it.

Industrial Designs protect the visual design or aesthetics of a product. Owning an industrial design means having exclusive rights to the appearance of your product.

Understanding Intellectual Property

Intellectual property refers to the legal rights granted to individuals or entities for their creations, including inventions, artistic works, literary pieces, and educational materials. These rights provide creators with exclusive control over the use and distribution of their creations, ensuring they can benefit from their efforts.

Educators are continually developing original teaching materials, such as lesson plans, worksheets, multimedia presentations, and even textbooks. These materials require significant time, effort, and creativity to produce. However, the ownership of these materials can become a complex issue when educators are employed by a school district or educational institution.

I made it a point to buy my own laptop, iPad, and iPhone. I also pay for Zoom, Canva, and Explain Everything. I did so because I want to own and control whatever content I create.

Owning your IP is important because it gives you control over how your creations are used, allows you to monetize your intellectual assets through licensing or sales, and provides legal protection against unauthorized use by others. It also enables you to enforce your rights through legal action if necessary.

The Importance of Ownership

Owning what you create allows you to be acknowledged and financially rewarded for your intellectual contributions. When you retain ownership, you have the potential to earn royalties, secure grants, and receive recognition for your work. This recognition not only boosts your professional standing but is also an awesome motivator to continue creating innovative teaching materials.

Ownership allows you to adapt and modify your materials as needed. Every classroom and student is unique, and educators often find it necessary to tailor their materials to suit specific teaching methods or student needs. By owning your creations, you can freely modify and adapt them without restrictions, ensuring your work product remains effective and relevant for your clients.

IP ownership encourages you to think of yourself as a business of one. To quote Jay Z, "I'm not a businessman; I'm a Business, man."

Examples from the Music Industry

When it comes to the significance of ownership, I get my inspiration from the music industry, where artists like Jay Z, Jermaine Dupri, and Master P have been consistent in their ownership rights to their creations. These artists not only own the record companies but also maintain control over their master recordings, publishing rights, and merchandise.

Jay Z, renowned for his business acumen, established his own record label, Roc-A-Fella Records, enabling him to control his music and build a successful empire. Similarly, Jermaine Dupri and Master P became pioneers in the industry by creating their labels, So So Def Recordings and No Limit Records, respectively. By owning their work, these artists were able to maximize their profits, negotiate favorable deals, and establish long-lasting legacies.

Applying IP Ownership to Education

Educators can apply the concept of ownership in education by purchasing their own tablets and laptops for creating educational materials. While schools often provide technology resources, it is essential for educators to have personal devices that they own outright.

By owning your devices, you can safeguard your intellectual property rights. When using school-provided equipment, there may be ambiguity regarding ownership and control over the materials created. Purchasing personal devices ensures that educators have full control over their work, reducing the risk of potential disputes or conflicts over ownership.

Personal devices also grant educators professional autonomy. When you own your technology purchases, you can choose the software, applications, and tools that best suit your needs and teaching style. This autonomy empowers you to stay up to date with emerging technologies and leverage them to enhance the learning experience for your students and potential clients.

Lastly, Intellectual Property ownership is essential for educators who want to monetize their talents.

Chapter 5

How To Talk About What You Do

"Create something people want to share."

— John Jantsch

As an edupreneur, creating content is key to building and growing your brand. But it's not always an easy journey. I know this from personal experience. When I first started creating content, I struggled to find my voice and figure out what my audience wanted to hear.

But over time, I learned that creating content is a process that requires patience, consistency, and a willingness to experiment and try new things.

One of the first steps in creating content is to identify your niche and what you want to be known for. This involves doing research and identifying gaps in the market that you can fill with your expertise. Once you've identified your niche, it's important to create a content strategy that aligns with your goals and resonates with your audience.

For me, creating content that is both educational and entertaining is key to engaging my audience. That's why I like podcasting, where I can be both informative and fun, using storytelling techniques to keep my audience hooked from start to finish.

Another important part of creating content is staying consistent. This means creating a schedule and sticking to it, whether that's posting a new video every week or publishing a blog post twice a month. Consistency helps build trust and credibility with your audience and keeps them coming back for more.

In discussing the realities of content creation for the edupreneur, Jade Weatherington captures the feeling, sharing:

"Educators provide a lot of free labor. I didn't want to labor unless I was getting paid. I quickly learned that, in the world of entrepreneurship, I was going to constantly work without pay. Of course, it was for the betterment of my business which was much different from not having a choice to be overworked without compensation. The extra work included making content for social media, developing new courses, planning monthly newsletters, and offering live webinars to attract and expand my new client base. Even though I was tired of offering free labor, I knew it was necessary to build my clientele. One way I did this was by offering free webinars and discounted courses. While I could have reduced the amount of time I worked, I didn't want to pay for a social media manager or marketing at the beginning of my business. So, I did the labor with the intent to get a return on my investment (ROI), with the investment being my time."

Of course, creating content is not without its challenges. There are times when I've struggled with coming up with the energy to interview folks or felt discouraged by low engagement numbers on my podcast. But during those times, I reminded myself of why I started creating content in the first place and the impact it has on my audience.

Ultimately, creating content as an edupreneur is about sharing your knowledge and expertise with the world, and inspiring others to learn and grow. It takes time, effort, and a willingness to learn and adapt, but the rewards are worth it.

CRAFTING COMPELLING CONTENT: UNLEASHING YOUR CREATIVITY AND IMPACTING AUDIENCES

Crafting compelling content for your business is a pivotal aspect of building a strong online presence and engaging your target audience.

It's about documenting your receipts. Meaning, you are sharing the work you are already doing. You are not pulling out random ideas to see what sticks.

The most important question to ask yourself: What do you want to be known for?

Then have an honest conversation with yourself about what kind of content resonates with your spirit and what kind of content you can consistently deliver.

Here's a section on how to create such content.

Creating Valuable Content

Almost everyone is connected to the internet, either by laptop, smartphone, or a tablet. Trying to get attention in this on-demand digital landscape, where attention spans are limited, is the aim of anything you post online. These internet streets are the gateway to sharing content that provides real value and allows you to stand out.

You want to start by understanding your audience's needs, pain points, and aspirations. Tailor your content to address these aspects, offering solutions, insights, or inspiration. Whether it's informative blog posts, engaging social media updates, or in-depth thinkpieces, make sure your content is relevant, informative, and helpful.

Video

Choosing video as the method of choice for content creation offers a multitude of advantages that can cater to various goals and preferences. Video combines visuals, audio, and motion to create a highly engaging and immersive experience. It can captivate viewers' attention and convey information more effectively than static text or images.

Video content can take various forms, such as tutorials, vlogs, webinars, interviews, animations, and documentaries. This versatility allows you to choose the format that best suits your message and target audience. Video is an excellent medium for storytelling. It allows you to create narratives, share personal experiences, and evoke emotions, making it easier to connect with viewers on a deeper level.

Video content is favored by search engines, leading to improved visibility and rankings in search results. Platforms like YouTube are search engines in themselves, making it easier for viewers to find your content. That said, video content often generates higher engagement rates compared to text or images on social media platforms. Viewers are more likely to like, comment, share, and interact with video content.

Lastly, video allows you to establish a personal connection with your audience. Viewers can see you and hear you, which builds trust and like-ability. Video content is accessible to a global audience, breaking down geographical barriers. This can be especially valuable for businesses and educators looking to reach a diverse and widespread audience, and video content can convey a lot of information in a relatively short amount of time. This can be particularly useful when trying to explain complex concepts concisely.

Written

Blogging and/or writing articles on LinkedIn or other publications is an invaluable tool in an edupreneur's content creation toolkit. It offers a dynamic platform for sharing knowledge, insights, and expertise with a global audience. Through blog posts/online articles, edupreneurs can establish themselves as thought leaders in their respective fields, building trust and credibility among their readers.

Blogs provide a space for in-depth exploration of educational topics, enabling edupreneurs to delve into subjects that matter most to their audience. Additionally, blogs facilitate ongoing engagement, as readers can leave comments, ask questions, and participate in discussions, creating a sense of community around the content.

Furthermore, blogging enhances an edupreneur's online visibility, improving search engine rankings and driving organic traffic to their educational resources. As a versatile medium, blogging can be a corner-stone of any successful edupreneurial venture.

Pictures and Graphics

The inclusion of pictures and graphics is an attention grabbing element in content creation for edupreneurs. Visual elements have the power to convey complex information succinctly and engage learners in ways that text alone cannot. Incorporating images, infographics, and diagrams into educational materials or shared online via social media can make complex concepts more digestible and accessible.

A dope visual can also pique interest and capture attention, attracting your target audience. Whether it's illustrating a blended learning station, simplifying a tutorial, or adding a touch of creativity to an otherwise tedious subject, pictures and graphics are indispensable tools that breathe life into content, making it more engaging and memorable to your audience.

Audio

When talking about content creation, audio has emerged as a powerful and flexible medium, with podcasts leading the way. Podcasts are audio recordings that can cover an array of topics, making them a valuable tool for edupreneurs. Here's why an edupreneur might choose to create a podcast:

Listeners can engage with your content while commuting, exercising, or doing household chores, allowing you to reach them during times when other forms of content may not be as convenient. Podcasts offer on-demand access, whereby listeners can choose when and where to consume your show, fitting it into their schedules seamlessly.

Your voice can establish a personal connection with your audience. Speaking directly to your listeners creates a sense of intimacy and authenticity, helping to build trust and rapport. Podcasts excel in storytelling. They allow you to narrate experiences, share anecdotes, and delve into topics with depth and nuance, making complex subjects more engaging and relatable.

Like video, podcasts come in various formats, including interviews, solo monologues, panel discussions, and narrative storytelling. The key is to select the format that best suits your objectives and personal style.

Please note that creating content is more than posting videos and memes on the internet. It's about using content to captivate your audience, whether they are students, teachers, or stakeholders, by making educational, entertaining, or social content that is relatable and memorable. Stories create an emotional connection that attracts your audience to the broader mission and vision of your company.

Storytelling with a Purpose

Stories have a unique power to dazzle and resonate with people. Weave storytelling into your content strategy, using narratives that align with your brand's mission and values. Craft stories that connect on an emotional level, illustrating how your product or service positively impacts lives. Storytelling adds depth and relatability to your brand, forging stronger connections with your audience.

Begin by defining the core narrative of your educational journey or that aha moment that called you to launch your business.

Some questions you may ask yourself:

- What inspired you to enter the field of education?
- What are your goals and values as an edupreneur?
- What unique experiences or insights do you bring to the table?
- What work speaks to your soul or core being?

A great edupreneur's story is a relatable narrative that blends vision, resilience, and authenticity. It begins with a clear and inspiring vision for a solution to a real-world problem. Your story showcases your determination and resilience, revealing your ability to adapt, learn from failures, and pivot when necessary. What truly will distinguish your story is your willingness to share not only triumphs but also vulnerabilities. Such stories inspire, resonate, and connect with audiences, transcending mere business success to impart valuable lessons and a sense of what is possible.

Consistency and Frequency

Consistency is key to maintaining your audience's interest and trust. Create a content calendar that outlines when and what type of content you'll publish. Whether it's daily social media updates, weekly blog posts, or monthly newsletters, stick to your schedule. Regularity builds anticipation and keeps your brand top-of-mind.

Consistent content keeps your audience engaged and interested. Irregular posting can lead to a loss of interest and a decrease in engagement. When you consistently deliver valuable content, you keep your audience coming back for more.

Consistency in style, tone, and messaging helps create a strong and recognizable brand identity. This makes it easier for your audience to identify your content, even when it's shared across various platforms.

Likewise, regular content keeps your brand or message in front of your audience. Being top of mind can be a significant advantage when potential customers or clients are making decisions. Additionally, regular postings or uploads lead to improvement. The more you create content, the better you become at it. Lastly, consistency allows you to refine your content creation process and deliver higher-quality materials.

Engagement and Interaction

Content shouldn't be a one-way street. Encourage interaction with your audience through comments, likes, shares, and discussions. Respond promptly and authentically to comments and messages.

Engaging with your audience not only strengthens your brand community but also provides valuable insights into their preferences and needs.

SEO Optimization

Here are some tips to get the most out of your content through SEO optimization.

- Optimize your content for search engines (SEO) to increase its discoverability. Identify relevant keywords and incorporate them naturally into your content, including titles, headings, and body text. Well-optimized content helps your business rank higher in search results, driving organic traffic.
- The goal of SEO is to increase organic traffic to a website by optimizing its content, structure, and other factors to align with search engine algorithms. For edupreneurs, SEO is crucial because it helps potential learners and customers discover their educational offerings and content online. Here are some best practices for edupreneurs:
- Conduct thorough keyword research to identify the terms and phrases potential learners are using to search for topics related to your educational offerings. Use tools like Google Keyword Planner or SEMrush to find relevant keywords with reasonable search volume and competition.
- Create high-quality, informative, and engaging content that addresses the needs and interests of your target audience. Content should be well-researched, up-to-date, and valuable to learners.
- Regularly update and refresh your content to keep it current and valuable. Add new insights, examples, or solutions within

your content bucket. This demonstrates consistency and
ensures that your content is relevant and up-to-date.

- Since you, as an edupreneur, will provide educational content,
  consider creating resources like guides, tutorials, and how-to
  articles that address specific niche-based needs. These can
  attract organic traffic and showcase your expertise.

Meet Valerie Lewis: Founder and CEO of P.I.T. Program

Valerie Lewis is an Assistant Principal, educational disruptor, and
entrepreneur.

Active in her community, Valerie is a member of the Gwinnett
Chamber of Commerce, Junior League of Gwinnett and North
Fulton Counties, Delta Kappa Gamma, and a sitting board
member of Fortitude Foundation, Inc. She immerses herself in
the community where she lives, works, and plays so this allows
her to build strong partnerships that offer value for multiple
stakeholders. She is also part of a large network of educators that
prides themselves on continuous learning, improving self, and
disrupting norms with solutions in tow.

This is her message for edupreneurs creating content for their
business:

"Make sure that the content that you are creating is good. There
are a lot of people who create social media content. There are a
lot of people who make money in the world. Very few people
know how to do both.

You have to make sure that you are leveraging tools and things that are available to you so that you can show up as the expert and you can actually make money, because you are not starting a business because you want to have an expensive hobby. That is not what we are doing here. We want to make sure that you're showing up online as an expert, as a leader.

When you're creating the content, make sure that the content that you create speaks to who you are, because a lot of the people that show up online, they see other people doing something, and do exactly what they're doing. They're just copying content, but what they cannot copy is an entire *ecosystem of a brand*."

———

DEFINING YOUR CONTENT CREATION BUCKET

We've given you a lot to think about when it comes to content creation. I want to close this section by stressing the importance of selecting content buckets or specific areas to create content in. Content buckets help maintain a clear focus and streamline your content creation efforts. When you have specific areas or themes to concentrate on, you can avoid content that might dilute your message or confuse your audience. It's about being intentional and strategic with your content.

Vanessa Lau, a popular content creator and business coach, recommends having three content buckets as part of her content strategy framework. While her specific recommendations may evolve over time, the concept of content buckets is a widely recognized strategy in content marketing.

So, why are content buckets so essential?

Content buckets provide a structured framework for creating and organizing content. Consistency in your content helps build trust with your audience, as they come to know what to expect from your brand. By focusing on specific areas or topics, you create a clear roadmap for your content creation journey. This not only streamlines your efforts but also makes it easier for your audience to follow along and know what to expect from you.

Focusing on specific content areas allows you to demonstrate your expertise and authority in those subjects. When you consistently create content within specific niches or themes, you position yourself as an authority in those areas. Over time, people start to recognize you as the go-to source for that particular type of content, which can be a game-changer for your brand.

And finally, content buckets can lead to deeper audience engagement. When you consistently provide valuable content in specific areas of interest, you're more likely to attract and retain a dedicated and engaged audience. By offering information to specific pain points within your niche, you can appeal to a broader range of people while still staying true to your core message. This diversity in content keeps your audience excited, engaged, and coming back for more.

So, whether you're a seasoned content creator or just starting out, remember that content buckets are your secret weapon for staying organized, establishing authority, and keeping your audience hooked.

CONTENT BUCKETS VISUAL

Sample of three content buckets with three content pillars.

Teaching with an LMS

Financial Literacy

Podcasting

EDUCATE

Share valuable information with your audience.

ENTERTAIN

Post content that is funny to amuse your followers.

RELATE

Show your audience that you understand their struggles.

In the graphic above, you see the three buckets that all of my content fall under. I added the content pillars to the graphic to identify the purpose of your content. Just like you wouldn't teach a lesson out of the blue, your content should have a direction or a why for what you're creating and sharing.

Content buckets and pillars are the foundational underpinnings of a brand's content strategy. They serve as the guiding principles that shape a company's messaging, allowing it to consistently convey its identity and values to its target audience. Together they are vital in maintaining brand coherence and building a strong online presence. By focusing on a few core themes and focusing on the purpose of the content, such as to educate, to entertain, or to relate, this strategy helps simplify content creation efforts, making it easier to generate high-quality and relevant material for various platforms.

This whole game boils down to you checking for the conversations that you love to have everyday and creating a business model around it.

What are some content buckets you might use? List them on the following page.

_____

_____

_____

_____

_____

_____

_____

_____

_____

_____

_____

_____

_____

_____

_____

_____

_____

_____

_____

_____

_____

Content That Converts: Harnessing the Power of a Lead Magnet

Have you ever visited a website and been asked to sign up to receive a free workbook, free webinar, or early access to a course? This is content that the individual is using to convert followers to buyers/customers, and these freebies can drive significant business growth. They can also serve as a powerful marketing tool and can attract and engage your target audience, allowing you to build, expand, and further reach a community of people who are genuinely interested in what you have to say and offer.

Content that converts provides valuable data and insights into audience behavior and preferences. You can use this data to refine your content strategy, optimize marketing efforts, and make informed decisions about your offerings. This is where having a lead magnet comes into play.

Lead Generation refers to the process of attracting and capturing potential customers or leads for a business. It involves using lead magnets, such as free educational resources or offers, to entice individuals to provide their contact information.

Lead Magnet

A lead magnet is a valuable free resource or enticing offer extended by a business to potential customers in exchange for their contact information, typically their email address. The primary objective of a lead magnet is to engage with potential customers and cultivate an email list. It serves as an incentive for visitors to willingly provide their contact details, thereby granting permission for follow-up through email marketing campaigns.

Lead magnets can encompass free ebooks, downloadable guides, cheat sheets, webinars, mini-courses, quizzes, templates, and more. The key lies in presenting something that directly addresses the needs or pain points of your target audience while also showcasing your expertise and unique selling proposition.

Think of how Teachers Pay Teachers offers you a free download in the hope of you becoming a paying customer.

This is an awesome example from EduMatch Publishing:

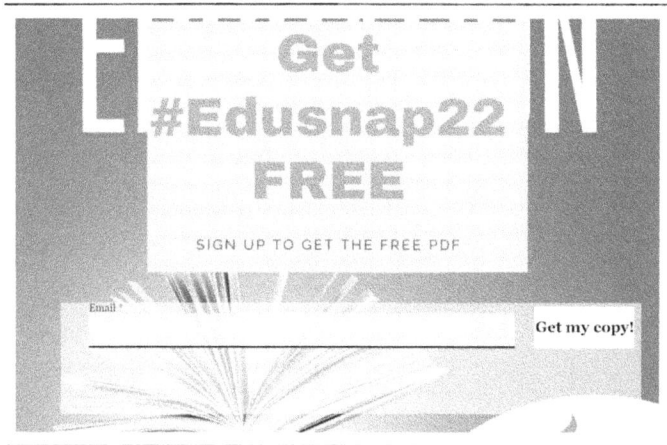

https://www.edumatch.org/edumatchpublishing/

For an edupreneur, possessing a lead magnet can yield significant benefits for several reasons.

Engagement

Lead magnets engage the target audience by furnishing solutions or sought-after information. This engagement can take the form of a live or pre-recorded webinar, for instance. Such interactions provide social proof, contributing to the development of trust and credibility. Consequently, it enhances the likelihood that leads or attendees will eventually become paying customers or clients.

Nurturing Relationships

Continuing with the webinar example, individuals may register for the webinar via a landing page or your website. The email addresses collected through these lead magnets empower you to foster relationships with people over time. Through email marketing efforts, such as sending guides or links to video tutorials, your business can consistently deliver additional value, education, and support.

Conversion

As leads receive valuable content and establish a rapport with your brand, they become increasingly predisposed to convert into paying customers or clients when presented with relevant offers. It's important not to be perceived solely as an influencer. The objective is to avoid being the individual with a massive following but struggling to persuade even a fraction of them to purchase your books or enroll in your coaching program.

In essence, a well-executed lead magnet is a powerful tool that not only engages and nurtures prospects but also drives conversion, ultimately solidifying your position as a valuable and influential figure in your field.

DATA COLLECTION

Recall the earlier example of registering for the webinar? The emails gathered during this process will form an email list, which comprises email addresses belonging to individuals or entities who have willingly subscribed to receive emails from a specific sender or organization. Email lists serve as a fundamental element of email marketing and communication strategies and are typically managed using email marketing software like ConvertKit.

These email lists contain valuable data, including contact information, interests, and preferences, which can be used to shape marketing strategies and create content that resonates with your audience.

With platforms such as ConvertKit, you can effortlessly create and host lead magnets directly within their system. This simplifies the process of delivering valuable content to new subscribers and effectively converts website visitors into leads. Additionally, you can orchestrate personalized email marketing campaigns by sending customized content and offers to different segments of your email list, enhancing the relevance of your messages.

Furthermore, ConvertKit offers comprehensive analytics on email open rates, click-through rates, and subscriber engagement. It seamlessly integrates with various other tools and platforms, such as landing page builders and e-commerce systems. This makes it a smart choice for edupreneurs looking to align their email marketing efforts with other facets of their business.

In summary, this entire process streamlines the creation and nurturing of customer relationships, and it's crucial never to overlook the inclusion of a compelling Call to Action.

A call to action (CTA) is a specific instruction or prompt designed to encourage an audience to take a particular action. CTAs are commonly used in various forms of content to guide the audience toward a desired outcome, such as signing up for a newsletter, making a purchase, sharing a post, or engaging in some other meaningful interaction. CTAs are important for content creators because they help drive engagement and conversions.

Here are some concrete examples of CTAs for content creators:

Subscribe to a Newsletter

- "Join our newsletter for weekly updates on [topic]. Click here to subscribe!"
- "Stay in the loop with our latest content. Sign up for our newsletter today."

Social Media Engagement

- "Like, share, and comment if you found this post helpful!"
- "Follow us for daily inspiration and tips."

Video Content

- "Don't forget to hit the 'Like' button if you enjoyed this video."
- "Subscribe to our channel to never miss an update!"

Ebook or Whitepaper Download

- "Download our free ebook on [topic] to level up your knowledge."
- "Get your hands on our latest whitepaper. Download now!"

Product Purchase

- "Shop now and get 20% off your first purchase. Limited time offer!"
- "Upgrade to the premium version today and unlock exclusive features."

Webinar or Event Registration

- "Reserve your spot for our upcoming webinar on [topic]."
- "Join us at our live event next week. Register here!"

Feedback and Surveys

- "We value your opinion. Take our quick survey and help us improve."
- "Leave feedback in the comments below and let us know your thoughts."

Contests and Giveaways

- "Enter our contest for a chance to win [prize]."
- "Don't miss out on our giveaway. Click here to participate!"

Lead Generation

- "Unlock exclusive content by filling out this short form."
- "Get a free consultation by providing your contact information."

Membership or Community Building

- "Join our exclusive community of [Microsoft professionals]."
- "Become a member today and access premium content."

CTAs should be clear, concise, and action-oriented, making it easy for your audience to understand what you want them to do. They can be placed strategically within your content, such as at the end of a blog post, in the middle of a video, or as a popup on your website, depending on the platform and format you're using. The choice of CTA depends on your goals and the type of content you're creating.

SALES STRATEGIES FOR TURNING YOUR TEACHERS SKILLS INTO DOLLAR BILLS

Now that your book is published, your course is designed, or your coaching/consulting program is ready to go, what happens next? I can tell you from personal experience that just because you build it, doesn't mean the customers will come. If you're not making sales, you don't have a business; you have an expensive hobby.

Selling yourself and your products or services are the lifeblood of your business. Whether you're a business owner or a freelancer, your endgame is to make money!

You gotta know who your ideal customers or clients are. Understanding their needs, preferences, and pain points is everything. Your mission is to tailor your message and offerings to resonate with your target audience.

Craft a thrilling and concise elevator pitch to convey your value within 30 seconds or less. When queried by decision-makers about your role, avoid stumbling or launching into a lengthy explanation. Practice your Elevator Pitch until it flows confidently and naturally.

Study other edupreneurs to discern their strengths and weaknesses. Emphasize what sets you apart, and refine your sales strategy with this knowledge.

When showcasing your products or services, clearly articulate how they address specific problems or fulfill distinct needs. Highlight their benefits and advantages.

Recognize that you're compensated for your expertise and experience, not merely your time. Price your offerings competitively, factoring in market conditions, expenses, and the value you provide. Avoid trading your time for money.

Edupreneurs can employ diverse strategies, such as webinars, podcasts, ebooks, and bundled offerings, to significantly boost their sales and impact in the educational market.

Webinars offer a dynamic platform to showcase your expertise and connect with potential clients. For instance, providing a free introductory webinar on a compelling topic can attract a broad audience, with opportunities to upsell premium courses or coaching services during the presentation.

Podcasts can serve as a content marketing tool, enabling edupreneurs to share valuable insights and establish thought leadership. Strategically integrate promotions for your books, products, or courses within podcast episodes to reach a dedicated audience seeking solutions to their problems.

Bundling courses or educational materials into comprehensive packages can be a potent sales tactic. For instance, if you offer individual courses on blended learning, consider bundling them into an A to Z blended learning "Masterclass" at a discounted rate to encourage investment in your expertise.

The following tools can be used individually or in combination to enhance sales efforts, improve customer engagement, and drive revenue growth for your businesses:

- **E-commerce Platforms:** Platforms like Shopify provide online storefronts, payment processing, and inventory management for businesses selling products or services online.
- **Sales Funnel and Landing Page Builders:** Platforms such as ClickFunnels and Leadpages help in creating optimized sales funnels and landing pages to convert website visitors into customers.
- **Customer Support and Helpdesk Software:** Solutions like Zendesk and Freshdesk enhance customer service and support, leading to better customer satisfaction and repeat business.
- **Chatbots and Live Chat Software:** Chatbots like Intercom and live chat tools like LiveChat offer real-time customer support and engagement, improving the overall customer experience.
- **Mobile Payment and Point-of-Sale (POS) Systems:** Mobile payment apps like Square enable businesses to accept payments and manage sales transactions efficiently. You can use Square to accept payments on the go such as when you're at conferences.

Staying on top of sales requires an approach that harnesses the power of technology and automation. The traditional methods of outreach, payment collection, distribution, and data management are no longer sufficient to meet the demands of modern consumers and edupreneurs when you can launch and build a business from a smartphone. Automation in sales, inventory, accounting, etc. has emerged as a game-changing solution, enabling organizations to simplify their processes, boost efficiency, and drive revenue growth.

By leveraging cutting-edge tools and intelligent software like Salesforce, you can focus your efforts on building relationships, nurturing leads, and delivering personalized experiences to customers. In this era of digital first, automation provides a myriad of benefits and practical applications such as invoice generation, sales and order processing, and payment collection, which has modernized the financial transaction process.

In the last section of the book, you learn more about automation and its relevance to empowering you as an edupreneur.

THE POWER OF AUTOMATION IN BUILDING YOUR BUSINESS

According to Chappel Billings, "When I started my consulting firm, my priority was to streamline administrative tasks so that I could focus more on advising clients. The turning point arrived when I incorporated automation into critical processes such as scheduling, document management, client communications, and data analysis. The advent of AI has further opened up possibilities for increased efficiency, allowing me to concentrate on forging high-impact strategic connections."

As previously mentioned, automation refers to the utilization of technology and software to streamline and mechanize repetitive tasks and processes. These automated systems can manage various facets of a business, encompassing email marketing, lead generation, customer onboarding, course enrollment, and more, all without the constant need for manual intervention.

I'm excited to share some concrete ways you can use automation to supercharge your business. Automation is like having your own virtual assistant, helping you streamline your processes, save time, and make your business run smoother than ever. Let's dive in!

Email Marketing Automation: Use tools like Mailchimp, ConvertKit, or ActiveCampaign to automate your email marketing. Set up email sequences, welcome emails, and follow-ups to nurture your subscribers and turn them into loyal customers. This way, you can focus on creating killer content while your emails do the work.

Social Media Scheduling: Platforms like Buffer or Hootsuite allow you to schedule your social media posts in advance. Plan your content calendar, write captions, and schedule posts for the week or month. It's a game-changer for maintaining a consistent online presence.

Chatbots for Customer Service: Implement chatbots on your website or social media to answer common customer inquiries 24/7. Tools like ManyChat or MobileMonkey can help you set up automated responses and provide instant support.

Sales Funnel Automation: Platforms like ClickFunnels or Kartra let you build and automate your sales funnels. Create landing pages, offer lead magnets, and guide your audience through a seamless buying process, all on autopilot.

CRM Systems: Customer Relationship Management (CRM) systems like HubSpot or Salesforce help you organize and automate your interactions with leads and customers. Track communications, set reminders, and personalize your outreach.

E-commerce Automation: If you're in e-commerce, tools like Shopify or WooCommerce can automate order processing, inventory management, and even customer reviews. Less manual work, more sales.

Content Distribution: Automate the distribution of your content using tools like MeetEdgar or Buffer. Share your blog posts, videos, or podcasts across various social platforms without manually posting every time.

Bookkeeping and Financial Automation: Software like QuickBooks or Xero can automate financial tasks like invoicing, expense tracking, and payroll, saving you hours of number-crunching.

Webinar and Online Course Automation: If you're into webinars or online courses, platforms like Teachable help automate registrations, reminders, and content delivery, allowing you to scale your audience effortlessly.

Workflow and Project Management: Use tools like Trello or Asana to automate project workflows. Assign tasks, set deadlines, and track progress in a visual and organized way.

Analytics and Reporting: Tools like Google Analytics or social media insights provide automated data on your website and social performance, helping you make data-driven decisions.

Explore AI Tools and Platforms Tailored for Startups

In education, AI is everywhere and you can't go to a conference or go anywhere online without hearing about its implementation or the implications of AI in the classroom. AI can also be used to automate systems and content creation for your business.

Many AI-as-a-Service (AIaaS) providers offer accessible and affordable solutions for tasks like data analysis, customer service chatbots, or predictive analytics.

To get started with AI tools for your business, you can begin by researching and identifying the areas of your business that could benefit from such automation. Once you have identified these areas, you can start exploring the various AI tools available in the market.

Data Collection and Utilization: Collect and organize data relevant to your business. AI thrives on data, so ensure you have a structured data collection process. Clean and organized data sets enable AI algorithms to produce more accurate insights. A tool like DataTurks is a data annotation platform that provides a suite of tools for data collection, annotation, and labeling.

AI for Efficiency: Use AI to automate repetitive tasks, streamline workflows, and boost operational efficiency. This could involve using AI-powered software for data analysis, content generation, inventory management, or optimizing marketing campaigns. A tool like Jasper helps users with content creation and generating images, and Descript uses machine learning to edit and transcribe videos.

Customer Engagement: Utilize AI to improve customer interactions. Implement chatbots or virtual assistants to provide instant support, personalize user experiences, and gather insights into customer preferences. A tool like Zendesk is a customer service platform that uses AI to help businesses improve their customer support.

AI is only going to get bigger and become a greater part of the work we do. Keep abreast of AI advancements and industry trends. Experiment with AI applications relevant to your business needs. Start small, test different AI tools, and scale the most effective ones.

Be sure to prioritize data security and ethical AI usage. Ensure compliance with regulations and prioritize customer privacy and data protection to build user trust.

Other tools to note: Microsoft Copilot, Open AI, and Chat GPT.

Remember, the key to successful automation is to set it up correctly and keep an eye on it. Automation isn't about "set and forget." It's about creating more time for what truly matters in your business while maintaining a personal touch. So go ahead and take advantage of these automation tools to level up your business.

Conclusion: The Edupreneur State of Mind

"The main thing is to keep the main thing the main thing."

— Stephen Covey

This edupreneur game is about love. You have to love the work. You can't be in it for the love of the people or for the love of the coin. It is important to focus on the impact of the work itself rather than external factors, such as the love of people or the desire for recognition.

Becoming an edupreneur is an exciting and rewarding journey that requires passion, creativity, and a commitment to lifelong learning. As we've explored in this book, there are many paths to success as an edupreneur, from starting a new company to launching a new product or service to writing a book.

Throughout this book, we've covered a wide range of topics, from identifying market opportunities to developing a business game plan and marketing your offerings. We've also discussed the importance of understanding your niche and developing your signature offer.

Above all, we've emphasized the importance of doing the work the right way for the right reasons. Whether you're developing a new technology platform, creating a new curriculum, or launching a new training program, your ultimate goal should always be to help learners achieve their full potential.

As an edupreneur, you have the power to make a real difference in the world of education. By taking risks, being innovative, and staying true to your values, you can create meaningful change and help shape the future of learning.

We hope that this book has provided you with the knowledge, tools, and inspiration you need to embark on your own edupreneurial journey. Remember, the road to success may be long and challenging, but with perseverance, passion, and a commitment to excellence, anything is possible.

While getting the coin and building a profitable and sustainable business is the goal, it is the passion for the work that ultimately drives success and personal fulfillment. If, after reading this book, you decide to go all in or if you're already in the game and have been inspired to go harder, make sure that you create a business that aligns with your ministry.

To quote The Notorious B.I.G., "Stay far from timid. Only make moves when your heart's in it. And live the phrase sky's the limit."

About the Author

Dr. Will Deyamport III

As seen on Forbes.com, Schoology Exchange, District Administration, EdSurge, iNACOL, and TechEdge magazine, Will Deyamport, III, Ed.D. is a District Instructional Technologist for Hattiesburg Public School District. Dr. Will, as he is better known as, specializes in assisting educators in going digital. In this role, he delivers in-person and virtual training, coaching, and designs and delivers online professional development courses and live webinars for teachers in grades K-12.

Additionally, Dr. Will is a podcaster, writer, documentary filmmaker, and educational consultant.

You can get your digital copy of The Edupreneur on Vimeo OnDemand.

Contributing Authors

Chappel Billings

An inspirational voice devoted to empowerment through education, Chappel Billings has motivated audiences nationwide with her authentic passion for creating transformative learning experiences. As a Director of Operations and Programs in the Worldwide Learning organization at a large tech company, Chappel spearheads initiatives at the intersection of technology and education. As the visionary Founder of the Grounded 44 Group, she was instrumental in supporting Women of Color, guiding them from conceptualization to the successful launch of their endeavors. Having presented at numerous local, state, and national conferences, Chappel advises learning and development professionals on leveraging technology and innovation strategies in L&D programming.

Chappel earned a B.S. in Special Education from Eastern Illinois University and an M.A. in School Leadership from Concordia University, Chicago. Chappel is currently completing her Ph.D. in Education Technology from Concordia University Chicago - her doctoral research explores Gen Z students' perceptions and experiences with learning management systems. Originally from Chicago but currently residing in Grand Prairie, Texas, Chappel derives inspiration and support from her husband and three daughters.

DR. ANDREA TERRERO GABBADON

Dr. Andrea Terrero Gabbadon is the founder and senior consultant at ILM Consulting Group, an equity-focused consultancy that offers professional learning and instructional coaching services. A former teacher and school leader in traditional public and charter schools, Andrea's work touches on culturally responsive and sustaining leadership practices, school organizational dynamics, and diversifying the teacher workforce. She is also a visiting assistant professor of educational studies at Swarthmore College. Andrea earned a B.S.Ed. in secondary education and Spanish from Temple University, a M.S.Ed. in school leadership from University of Pennsylvania, and a Ph.D. in policy and organizational studies with an emphasis on urban education from Temple University. More importantly, she is a wife, mother, engaged community member, and a coffee enthusiast.

Valerie C. Lewis

Valerie Lewis is dedicated to the transformation of learning through engaging and creative activities for ALL students. Today's classroom should reflect the desires of students in order to prepare them for careers and beyond. She grew up in Miami, FL and graduated with a Bachelor's in Elementary Education from Oakwood University, a Master's in Special Education from Howard University, and an Ed.S. in Leadership from Liberty University. She currently resides in Metro Atlanta and is a wife, mother of 3 beautiful souls, and a high school administrator.

Her belief is that critical learning possibilities should be activated NOW in order to prepare students for skills that will make them future ready. This will enable them to compete on a global scale! Students need to lift their voice and advocate for themselves, but this skill should be modeled and taught explicitly and consistently. Lessons should be personalized and student-centered, and not mainly based upon the teacher's ideals and comforts. In this manner, cater to a variety of learning styles. Valerie is an encourager and motivator and has the mentality that the TEAM is better together.

In order to strengthen the team, she understands that learning MUST create IMPACT. The formula should always be ONE SIZE FITS...ONE! She continues on her mission to show that learning is a daring lifelong journey but ultimately...TRANSFORMS.

SHELLY SANCHEZ TERRELL

Shelly Sanchez Terrell (@ShellTerrell) is an award winning digital innovator, international speaker, and author of various education technology books. She has trained teachers in over 20 countries as a guest expert, consultant, and ambassador for the U.S. Embassy. She was named Woman of the Year by the National Association of Professional Women and received a Bammy Award as the founder of #Edchat. She has been recognized by several entities as a leader in the movement of teacher driven professional development as the founder and organizer of various online conferences, Twitter chats, and webinars. She currently teaches in Texas and is the author of TeacherRebootcamp.com, Hacking Digital Learning with Edtech Missions, The 30 Goals Challenge for Teachers, and Learning to Go.

Dr. Tracy Timberlake

Dr. Tracy Timberlake is a Multi-Award Winning Money Mindset Business Coach, Speaker, and Online Influencer. In the last 7 years, she has built not one, but two multimillion-dollar businesses and teaches her clients to do the same by focusing on methods that help them break out of the middle-class money mentality and elevate to a place of conscious wealth creation. Recipient of the prestigious Miami 40 Under 40, she has spoken on the TEDX stage, been featured on NBC, CBS, Entrepreneur Magazine, etc. It's no wonder her clients appropriately titled her "The Entrepreneur Whisperer." To date, over 15,000 people have taken her online courses, workshops, and trainings.

Dr. Tracy is also Co-founder of Flourish Media and the Flourish Media Conference whose claim to fame is an annual event where they introduce women-owned businesses to potential investors for seed-funding of up to $15,000,000. She also serves on the Executive Team of the Brook Church Miami and as an Adjunct Professor at Trinity International University. A native of Miami, Dr. Tracy Timberlake earned a Doctorate in Education from Nova Southeastern University, a Master of Arts from John Brown University, and a Bachelor in Business Administration from the illustrious University of Miami (Go 'Canes!).

JADE WEATHERINGTON, M.ED

Jade Weatherington, M.Ed serves as the CEO and Founder of Teacher Jade's Writing Academy. With fifteen years of online teaching experience, she transformed her side hustle of teaching online into a thriving business following her departure from a traditional teaching role. Beyond her academy, she also guides aspiring entrepreneurs in creating, marketing, and selling online resources.

EduMatch

PUBLISHING

www.ingramcontent.com/pod-product-compliance
Lightning Source LLC
Chambersburg PA
CBHW040926210326
41597CB00030B/5198